W9-AYK-759

The Science and Technology of BASEBALL

Other titles in *The Science and Technology of Sports* series include:

The Science and Technology of Basketball

The Science and Technology of Football

The Science and Technology of Hockey

The Science and Technology of Soccer

The Science and Technology of Track & Field

The **Science** and
Technology of
Sports

The **Science** and **Technology** of **BASEBALL**

John Allen

ReferencePoint
Press

San Diego, CA

© 2020 ReferencePoint Press, Inc.
Printed in the United States

For more information, contact:
ReferencePoint Press, Inc.
PO Box 27779
San Diego, CA 92198
www.ReferencePointPress.com

LIBRARY OF CONGRESS CATALOGING-IN-PUBLICATION DATA

Name: Allen, John, 1957– author.
Title: The Science and Technology of Baseball/by John Allen.
Description: San Diego, CA: ReferencePoint Press, Inc., 2020. | Series: The Science and Technology of Sports | Audience: Grades: 9 to 12. | Includes bibliographical references and index.
Identifiers: LCCN 2018060656 (print) | LCCN 2019005834 (ebook) | ISBN 9781682826485 (eBook) | ISBN 9781682826478 (hardback)
Subjects: LCSH: Baseball—Juvenile literature. | Sports sciences—Juvenile literature. | Baseball—Statistical methods—Juvenile literature.
Classification: LCC GV867.5 (ebook) | LCC GV867.5 . A45 2020 (print) | DDC 796.357—dc23
LC record available at https://lccn.loc.gov/2018060656

CONTENTS

Introduction   6
  A Game of Numbers

Chapter One   10
  Statcast and the Data Revolution

Chapter Two   22
  Making Pitchers More Effective

Chapter Three   34
  A Scientific Approach to Batting

Chapter Four   45
  Applying Science to Fielding and
  Baserunning

Chapter Five   56
  Using Science to Avoid Injuries

Source Notes   67
For Further Research   72
Index   74
Picture Credits   79
About the Author   80

A Game of Numbers

In the fifth game of the 2018 National League Championship Series, Milwaukee Brewers manager Craig Counsell made a highly unusual move. He pulled his starting pitcher, left-hander Wade Miley, after Miley walked the first batter on five pitches. Counsell was not upset with Miley. In fact, he planned to take him out after only one batter. Miley was a decoy. By starting a left-handed pitcher, Counsell knew Los Angeles Dodgers manager Dave Roberts would stack his lineup with right-handed batters. According to statistics, Roberts's right-handed batters were great against lefties, but not nearly so good against right-handed pitchers. When Counsell replaced Miley with right-hander Brandon Woodruff, he knew he was placing the Dodgers at a disadvantage. "Look, they're trying to get matchups, we're trying to get matchups,"[1] Counsell told reporters afterward. In the numbers game that is modern baseball, Counsell was using advanced analytics to play the percentages.

Mountains of Data

Counsell, like other managers in Major League Baseball (MLB), uses a scientific method called analytics to help win games. Analytics is the process of finding patterns in data to aid in making better decisions. For a baseball manager, this means decisions about when to take a pitcher out of the game or which pinch hitter to send to the plate in the ninth inning. Baseball is well suited to analytics because it produces lots of data for each game—as in *mountains* of data, about hits, runs, pitches, catches, swings, misses, and every other action that takes place inside the ballpark. Front offices in baseball swear by the new data-driven approach, making it key to their hiring practices. According to Chicago Cubs manager Joe Maddon, "If guys coming up don't want to accept analytics, numbers and methods in that regard, you pretty much eliminate your chance of becoming a major-league manager."[2]

analytics
A systematic search for patterns in data and statistics

Dating back more than a century, baseball has always gone hand in hand with a fascination for numbers. Even casual baseball fans can name Babe Ruth's career home run total (714), Hank Aaron's even larger total (755), and Joe DiMaggio's record of consecutive games with a hit (56). For decades, managers and teams evaluated players according to a few basic statistics, such as batting average (number of hits divided by number of at bats), runs batted in (number of runs scored from hits), and earned run average (the average number of runs allowed by a pitcher per nine innings). But with the arrival of computers and sophisticated data analysis, these basic stats gave way to dozens of new statistical tools, such as wins above replacement and on-base plus slugging percentage. The new tools provide a clearer picture of which skills and strategies are most effective in winning baseball games.

Adding to the trove of data is the input from digital technology. Ballparks today are equipped with sophisticated cameras and radar that enable teams to compile all sorts of data about each play in a game, from how much a curveball breaks (deviates from a straight path) to how far an outfielder must sprint to snag a fly ball. Teams analyze this data in order to exploit the strengths of their own players and the weaknesses of opponents. Statcast, the MLB service that compiles all this information, stores more than 17 petabytes of data in one season. This is equivalent to more than 226 years of video.

Milwaukee Brewers pitcher Brandon Woodruff throws a pitch during a game in 2018. By using a scientific method called analytics, MLB managers can find patterns in game data that help them decide when to change pitchers or which pinch hitter to send to the plate.

Big Changes for Longtime Fans

For longtime fans, the results of teams using analytics on the field can be startling. For example, defensive players may station themselves on one side of the field and leave the other side mostly open. This is because data tells them where a certain batter is most likely to hit the ball. Managers may change pitchers five or six times during the game in an attempt to get the statistical matchups they want. More batters may swing from their heels, trying to launch the ball into the air and increase their chances of hitting for extra bases. Striking out, once considered a cringeworthy failure, now is accepted with a shrug.

All this strategy causes games to last longer, often extending to four hours. In 2017, MLB games averaged three minutes and forty-eight seconds between balls put in play. Some worry that younger fans, accustomed to more action-packed sports like football and basketball, might tune out the new version of baseball. "The sport is going down a path that is a byproduct of very smart people figuring out the best strategies to win," says San Francisco Giants chief executive Larry Baer. "What's the impact on the consumers that are watching?"[3]

Nonetheless, MLB continues to collect billions in ticket sales and TV revenue for its technology-driven product. Often the science of analytics dovetails perfectly with great athletic skill. This was the case in the ninth inning of the 2018 American League Championship Series game between the Boston Red Sox and the Houston Astros. Down two runs with two outs and the bases loaded, Astros' hitter Alex Bregman sent a screaming line drive into left field. Positioned according to analytics, Boston left fielder Andrew Benintendi was in the right place to make the catch. However, the ball was sinking fast, and Benintendi had to make a snap decision. He dove headlong, caught the ball an inch off the turf, and secured the victory for the Red Sox. It took science plus the human element to produce one of the season's most memorable plays.

CHAPTER ONE

Statcast and the Data Revolution

Fans attending the September 5, 2018, game between the hometown Colorado Rockies and the San Francisco Giants saw baseball history being made. That night Rockies shortstop Trevor Story hit three home runs in the thin, mile-high atmosphere of Denver's Coors Field. On the first homer, Story swung so hard he fell down and almost missed seeing the ball as it sailed over the left field wall. What was historic was the length of Story's second blast. According to Statcast, MLB's data-collection system, it was the longest home run ever measured by scientific means. The towering shot traveled 505 feet (154 m), striking a concourse far beyond the left field fence and bouncing into a distant concession stand. Even Story's veteran teammates were impressed. "I knew that was close to 500 feet," says outfielder Carlos González. "As soon as it came off the bat, I was like, 'Oh my God, it's going to hit the scoreboard.' . . . It was awesome."[4] And due to the Statcast sensors and radar mounted throughout the ballpark, Story's historic home run could be broken down in greater detail than was ever possible before.

An Automated Tracking System

In an age of data-driven professional sports, Statcast collects dizzying amounts of data about every play in every MLB game. This high-speed, automated tracking system uses state-of-the-art radar and digital cameras to measure the speed of pitches, the distance of hits, the reaction times of fielders, and hundreds of other aspects of the game. Each game creates more raw data than is added to the Library of Congress web archive every month. MLB makes most of this data available online not only to teams but to broadcasters and ordinary fans. Long-suffering fans now have science-based reasons to bellyache about their team's performance.

Statcast can make past methods of de-scribing baseball games seem out of date. For example, Story's record-breaking home run once would have been dismissed with a few ba-sic facts. It was a one-ball and one-strike count, and Giants pitcher Andrew Suárez delivered a fastball. However, Statcast was able to reveal much more. Suárez threw a four-seam fastball (a specialty pitch that seems to rise) that zipped in at 92 miles per hour (148 kph). Story had about 0.4 seconds to decide where the ball was and whether to swing. Once struck, the ball had an exit velocity off Story's bat of 111.9 miles per hour (180 kph), well in the range of the best power hitters. To hit the ball high into the air, Story swung the bat with a vertical launch angle of 28 degrees, which is a healthy uppercut. According to Statcast data, Story maximized his swing potential. He hit the ball hard, high, and far. For players like Story, Statcast can be a helpful guide to what is really going on in a baseball game. "It's cool," says Daniel Murphy, formerly of the Chicago Cubs and now with the Colorado Rockies, "because with all the data we've been given now, [we have] some of the answers to the test."[5]

After a trial run in 2014, MLB spent tens of millions of dollars to install Statcast in all thirty MLB stadiums the following year. In es-sence, Statcast is a combination of two tracking systems. One is a TrackMan Doppler radar setup that each ballpark has installed in an elevated spot behind home plate. This advanced radar tracks nearly every motion of the baseball at twenty thousand frames per second. (Pop-ups and weak groundouts sometimes escape

sensors
Devices that detect and respond to information from the physical world

11

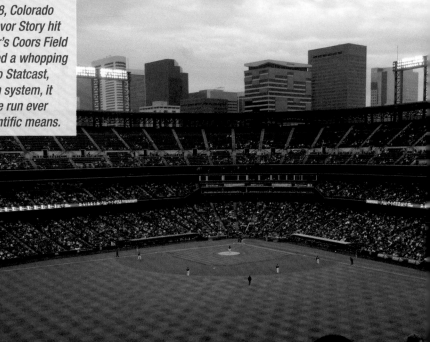

On September 5, 2018, Colorado Rockies shortstop Trevor Story hit a home run at Denver's Coors Field (pictured) that traveled a whopping 505 feet. According to Statcast, MLB's data-collection system, it was the longest home run ever measured using scientific means.

tracking.) The radar system records pitch speed, exit velocity, launch angle, and batted ball distance, as with the Story home run. It also yields more exotic data, such as spin rate of pitches and arm strength of pitchers and fielders. The other tracking system is a battery of six high-resolution stereoscopic cameras, deployed in banks of three cameras apiece along each foul line. The camera system tracks every movement of the players on the field. This enables teams to measure player speed, distance traveled, direction taken, and other movements for each play. Combined, the two systems provide a treasure trove of data to evaluate player performance and develop team strategies.

Changing the Game with Data

Statcast, with its high-tech hardware, is only the latest example of baseball's love affair with data and statistics. The first big push toward data analysis in baseball began in the late 1970s. It was driven by two factors. First was the rapid advance of computer technology, allowing for high-speed analysis of all kinds of statistics. Second was the astonishing rise of baseball salaries, with the top stars demanding, and getting, millions for their services. With so much money invested in their rosters, MLB teams were desperate for new ways to gain an advantage over their opponents. They needed to keep paying customers flowing through the turnstiles. Like other businesses, the ball clubs needed statistical analysis in order to become more efficient. And the man who showed the way was a baseball fanatic living in Lawrence, Kansas, named Bill James.

stereoscopic
Relating to a process in which two images from different angles are combined to give the illusion of depth

James believed that most baseball statistics were misleading numbers that measured the wrong things. According to business journalist Michael Lewis, "The statistics were not merely inadequate; they lied. And the lies they told led the people who ran major league baseball teams to misjudge their players, and mismanage their games."[6] For example, James pointed out that errors—or fielding miscues—were always considered evidence that a player was a poor fielder. But to make an error, a fielder first had to get to the ball. Faster players with more range might make a few more errors because they could get to more balls than slower players. Yet they still were more valuable fielders because over the course of a season, they would make more plays and record more outs. The old statistic about errors could make a slow, mediocre fielder look better than he really was. The more important measurement was a player's range.

James applied this type of thinking to all kinds of statistics. He pointed out that the difference between a .300 hitter—star level in the big leagues—and a slightly above-average .275 hitter was only one more hit every two weeks. So was it worth paying lots of money for so few extra hits? He stressed the importance of on-base percentage (hits, walks, and hit-by-pitch divided by times at bat) versus batting average, arguing that a walk was as good as a hit—an idea familiar to every Little Leaguer. James found that getting on base a lot and getting more bases per hit resulted in a team scoring more runs. And after all, producing runs, not hits, was the main goal. To prove his point, he created a new statistic called OPS, combining on-base percentage with slugging percentage. The latter measures a batter's ability to hit doubles, triples, and home runs. James believed that OPS was more valuable than batting average in comparing player performance. In fact, he began to develop several new statistics, such as runs created, to more accurately define what matters in winning baseball games. James called his analysis system sabermetrics, from the acronym of the Society for American Baseball Research (SABR), of which he was a proud member.

A Test for Sabermetrics

From his outpost in Kansas, James published his findings in a sixty-eight-page photocopied booklet he called *1977 Baseball Abstract: Featuring 18 Categories of Statistical Information That You Just Can't Find Anywhere Else*. His first *Baseball Abstract* included a few pages of explanation followed by page after page of tiny numbers in rows and columns. Although it sold only seventy-five copies, the book attracted enough attention from hard-core statisticians to encourage James to continue his pursuit. Eventually, his annual *Baseball Abstract* reached the eyes of big league management.

statistician
An expert in gathering and interpreting statistics

Statcast collects vast amounts of data about every play in every MLB game. This high-speed, automated tracking system uses state-of-the-art radar and digital cameras (pictured) to measure the speed of pitches, the distance of hits, and hundreds of other aspects of the game.

It took more than twenty-five years, but finally an MLB team adopted James's data-based recipe for success. The Oakland Athletics (often called the A's) were a successful franchise that had to make do with one of baseball's lowest payrolls. When the A's lost two of their best players to free agency before the 2002 season, general manager Billy Beane decided to test James's ideas as a way to get more out of the team's low-budget roster. For example, to replace slugging first baseman Jason Giambi, the A's acquired three affordable players with special skills that were undervalued. As Lewis explains:

[Beane] couldn't and wouldn't find another Jason Giambi; but he could find the pieces of Giambi he could least afford to be without, and buy them for a tiny fraction of the cost of Giambi himself. The A's front office had broken down Giambi into his obvious offensive statistics—walks, singles, doubles, home runs—along with his less obvious ones—pitches seen per plate appearance, walk to strike-out ratio—and asked: which can we afford to replace? And they realized that they could afford, in a roundabout way, to replace his most critical offensive trait, his on-base percentage, along with several less obvious ones.[7]

One key acquisition was an obscure player named Scott Hatteberg. A former catcher with a bad arm, Hatteberg came cheap, and with his excellent batting eye, he got on base a lot. He could make up for a good part of Giambi's on-base percentage. The A's taught Hatteberg to play first base and learned to live with his defensive limitations. Led by several players like Hatteberg whose hidden talents fit James's sabermetric approach, the A's, after a rocky start, began to win games. In the last month of the season, the A's ripped off twenty wins in a row, an American League record. For the twentieth victory, the game-winning home run was struck by Scott Hatteberg.

The Spread of Moneyball

In 2003 Lewis published *Moneyball: The Art of Winning an Unfair Game*. In the book, he described James's scientific approach to statistics and how the Oakland Athletics had employed his ideas to get maximum value for the team's limited budget. *Moneyball* caused a sensation in the sport. Several teams set about implementing their own versions of the system. The Boston Red Sox were so impressed that they tried to hire Beane themselves.

Meanwhile, certain old-school managers, scouts, and front office veterans scoffed at the book. They insisted that building a team and playing winning baseball required experience and savvy, not a degree in computer science. Scouts in particular objected to the Moneyball theory, which seemed to replace their judgment on

A Market for Baseball Data

MLB teams are hungry for data to feed their analytics approach to devising strategy and evaluating talent. Their major source for data is MLB Advanced Media, the $15 billion company that operates Statcast and MLB.TV. Every morning, MLB Advanced Media delivers data bundles to all thirty teams. These bundles include Statcast data, play-by-play files from the previous night's games, and updates on player contracts and injuries. However, the bundles satisfy only part of the teams' data needs. MLB ball clubs also rely on outside sources to provide them with even more statistical information.

For example, companies like Baseball Info Solutions and Inside Edge maintain a thriving business selling data to MLB teams. These firms deploy an army of video scouts to record all sorts of details about every major league game. Teams are happy to pay for this data, since it costs less than paying staff members to compile the same kinds of charts. Outside data vendors allow teams to focus their resources on analyzing data instead of gathering it. Graham Goldbeck, who is manager of data analytics and operations at Sportvision, which runs PITCHf/x, says these outside companies provide a valuable service. "There are other companies where they collect data and just put it in an easy-to-understand form and deliver to teams," says Goldbeck. "It's easier to pay that person a one-time fee, [instead of] having to have someone on staff go through and figure out how to do all that when they could be doing other stuff."

Quoted in R.J. Anderson, "The Surprising Places MLB Teams Get Their Information from in the Post Moneyball Era," CBS Sports, March 7, 2017. www.cbssports.com.

talent with a slide-rule approach. Many longtime scouts insisted that it took a practiced eye to evaluate young players and decide which ones had the greatest potential. Some critics also pointed out that much of the A's success in 2002 had nothing to do with James's methods of analysis. The A's already had three first-rate young starting pitchers (barely mentioned in Lewis's book) who placed them among the top contenders in the American League.

Nonetheless, the concept of sabermetrics spread to all the other MLB franchises. Teams began to rethink strategy in many areas, from batting order and bullpen usage to sacrifice bunts and

A group of scouts use radar guns to evaluate prospective players. Many longtime scouts believe that it takes a practiced eye, not statistics, to decide which players have the greatest potential.

stolen bases. Some teams without Oakland's budget constraints thrived on the new ideas. When the Red Sox hired twenty-eight-year-old Theo Epstein, he became the youngest general manager in baseball history. Epstein was a strategy wonk who was devoted to analytics. According to business reporter Tom Ward, "Epstein has believed in [analytics] since he was a kid reading Bill James' *By the Numbers*, a statistical analysis of major league players. While with the Red Sox, he sent interns to the NCAA [National Collegiate Athletic Association] headquarters to search through 30 years of stats to see if there were any trends to becoming a successful major leaguer."[8] Like Beane, Epstein used data analysis to take advantage of the inefficient market for players in the big leagues. In 2004 he even put James on the payroll as a consultant. That same season the Red Sox came back from a 0–3 deficit to defeat the New York Yankees for the American League pennant and went on to win the World Series for the first time in eighty-six years.

From Sabermetrics to Statcast

With MLB teams committed to data analysis, all that remained was to increase the amount of data available. Digital technology provided new ways to compile information about each pitch in a baseball game. In 2007 MLB installed a pitch-tracking system called PITCHf/x in every major league ballpark. PITCHf/x, the forerunner of Statcast, consisted of two cameras mounted inside the stadium. It recorded the speed of a pitch at its release point, its speed as it crossed the plate, and the break of the ball as it moved toward the catcher. Although less sophisticated compared to Statcast, PITCHf/x established MLB's commitment to gathering all sorts of data about the inner workings of a baseball game.

At the same time, experts in data analysis were building on James's pioneering efforts. Nate Silver, who is widely known today for his data-based forecasts of election results, made a key contribution to baseball research. He invented a system for predicting player performance based on sabermetric principles. Called PECOTA, for Player Empirical Comparison and Optimization Test Algorithm, Silver's system uses a vast amount of data to predict final stats for players and the number of wins their ball clubs would achieve. PECOTA compares each player's career statistics against a database of more than twenty thousand major league player statistics dating back to World War II. PECOTA has proved to be remarkably accurate in its forecasts of certain individual categories, such as OPS and ERA (earned run average), but less accurate for team performance.

Today each team has its own department of data analysis to deal with the flood of information provided by Statcast and other

The Lessons of Moneyball and Analytics

Baseball's embrace of data analysis has spread to other sports and even to non-sports uses. For example, teams in the National Basketball Association (NBA) employ statistical research to design their strategies. The Golden State Warriors have led the way with their use of analytics, machine learning, and data science. The Warriors, winners of three of the last four NBA championships, used data analysis to determine that almost all their shots should be taken either from beyond the 25-foot (7.6 m) 3-point line or within a few feet of the basket. By avoiding inefficient midrange shots, the Warriors maximized their offensive talents. Following the Warriors' lead, many NBA teams now shoot forty or more 3-point shots a game.

A more surprising proponent of the analytics approach is the US military. The principles of Moneyball are taught at the School of Advanced Military Studies at Fort Leavenworth, Kansas, and at the US Marine Corps base in Quantico, Virginia. Like Billy Beane with the Oakland Athletics, military teachers tout the use of statistics to predict outcomes. They also urge their students to question old practices and be open to new, more efficient methods. According to Colonel Gregory Fontenot, director of the University of Foreign Military and Cultural Studies, "What we liked about *Moneyball* is that on the face of it, they looked at baseball and said, 'The things we believe we know are based on mistaken premises, and if we take a look at baseball differently, we will see solutions we would not see.'"

Quoted in Marc Tracy, "Military 'Moneyball,'" *New Republic*, February 28, 2013. www.newrepublic.com.

sources. Expert statisticians work long hours combing through databases and tweaking computer simulations to come up with a slight competitive edge for their team. Houston Astros' general manager Jeff Luhnow swears by analytics, having used it to bring his ball club from the bottom of the American League to the 2017 World Series championship. "We have so much technology around the ballpark," says Luhnow, "and information about the trajectory of the ball, the physics of the bat swing, the physics and the biomechanics of the pitcher's delivery. . . . It's, quite frankly, overwhelming in terms of the amount of information that we have access to and intimidating to figure out how to analyze all that information."[9]

When he first published his ideas about statistics and baseball strategy, Bill James could not have imagined how technology, from computers to digital cameras and radar, would help revolutionize the game. But science and technology cannot take the place of the human element. In November 2018 James, still a consultant with the Boston Red Sox, drew fire for a controversial comment. "If the players all retired tomorrow," James wrote on Twitter, "we would replace them, the game would go on; in three years it would make no difference whatsoever. The players are NOT the game, any more than the beer vendors are."[10] MLB management and the Red Sox were quick to reject James's words. For fans of the Boston Red Sox—for nearly all baseball fans—numbers and sophisticated analysis can never replace the beauty of a Mookie Betts home run swing or a Chris Sale strikeout pitch. Baseball will never be purely a numbers game.

CHAPTER TWO

Making Pitchers More Effective

Edwin Diaz, the Seattle Mariners' all-star relief pitcher, credits his bullpen coach Brian DeLunas with a good deal of his success. DeLunas studies Diaz's pitching motion in minute detail. He looks for changes in his windup and delivery. He watches Diaz warm up and reminds him to keep his weight back and not rush his throwing motion to the plate. "Every time, when I'm warming up, I like for him to step behind me," says Diaz. "When I'm doing something badly, he lets me know quick. That's what I like."[11] Yet DeLunas is a rarity in MLB. He is a coach who has never thrown or hit a professional pitch. He has become a valuable member of the Mariners' coaching staff because of his expertise in biomechanics, the science of the body's structure and movement. He strives to keep the Mariners' pitchers in tune to the precise motion of their pitching deliveries.

Improving Pitching with Biomechanics

Like other MLB teams, the Seattle Mariners are using a combination of biometric training and data analysis to help their pitchers do their job more effectively. Pitching is a fine art in baseball. It calls for a rhythmical windup; a coiling of back, hip, and leg muscles; a powerful stride and shift of weight; a smooth arm motion at a precise angle for speed and control; and a balanced follow-through. Throwing curveballs and sliders adds more difficulty to the procedure. According to Dr. Glenn Fleisig at the American Sports Medicine

Institute, the shoulder rotation of a baseball pitcher is the fastest motion of any joint in any athlete. A hundred things can go wrong. A faulty throwing motion puts a tremendous amount of strain on a pitcher's shoulder and elbow. Hurlers who are paid millions of dollars are always one pitch away from injury and a long stay on the disabled list. That is why experts like DeLunas who can draw on the latest science in their coaching are so much in demand today.

DeLunas was a promising pitcher in high school until his shoulder popped while he was throwing a curveball. With his playing days over, he drifted into college coaching, where he became interested in biomechanics. He began to use biomechanical analysis to study how a pitcher's body moves through the throwing motion. He looked for subtle changes that could cause problems for a pitcher's ability to throw with speed and accuracy. In 2014 DeLunas joined with a business partner to open Premier Pitching and Performance (P3) in St. Louis, Missouri. P3 has used new technologies to offer instruction in pitching performance and strength training for players from high school to the major leagues. The company has drawn on experts in physical therapy, massage therapy, and chiropractic care. DeLunas has also incorporated holistic methods in P3, addressing psychological and emotional well-being as well as physical health.

DeLunas's work with Seattle pitcher David Phelps drew such a positive response from Phelps and his agent that the Mariners' front office summoned DeLunas for an interview. General manager Jerry Dipoto ended up hiring him as bullpen coach. "We view Brian as a connector," says Dipoto. "Taking the bio-mechanical view of a pitcher, connecting with the analytical view, connecting again with the

The Seattle Mariners use a combination of biometric training and data analysis to help their pitchers do their job more effectively. All-star pitcher Edwin Diaz (pictured) credits bullpen coach Brian DeLunas, an expert in biomechanics, with much of his success.

emotional and psychological angle and then how to reach players in today's times. . . . He's an easy communicator and understands the game at a variety of angles."[12]

Motion Analysis of a Pitcher's Delivery

Services like P3 and the Micheli Center for Sports Injury Prevention use state-of-the-art technology to break down and study a pitcher's throwing motion. This includes methods such as 3-D motion analysis. At the Micheli Center in Waltham, Massachusetts, a client is first measured for height and weight and tested for basic flexibility. A yoga class might be recommended if the person demonstrates joint stiffness or problems with range of motion. Next a team of engineers fits the client's body with fifty sensors from ankles to fingertips. The sensors look like small gray Ping-Pong balls. After stretching briefly, the client begins to throw baseballs from an Astroturf mound into a net 50 feet (15.2 m) away. Once the warm-up is complete, the client is handed a special ball with its own sensor. The person then proceeds to throw different kinds of pitches—fastballs, curveballs, changeups—with varying levels of effort. For each pitch, a set of ten motion-tracking cameras mounted on the walls tracks the Ping-Pong balls on the client's body at 240 frames per second. This results in a 3-D version of the client's throwing motion, which can be analyzed on a computer screen in great detail.

A week or two later, the client returns to get the results. Sarah Jarvis, a Micheli bioengineer, explains how the software uses the client's height and weight to calculate the proper joint angles and torque (or twisting force) for his or her body type. Jarvis goes into variables such as release point, or where the ball is released; trunk tilt, or the angle of the torso during the throwing motion; and hip separation, or the rotation of the lower body toward home plate before turning the shoulder and trunk. Hip separation is especially important for throwing a fastball, since it creates a powerful slingshot effect for the throwing arm.

Biomechanics services like P3 also offer force plate testing for pitchers. A force plate is an electronic platform that measures the distribution of force as a pitcher's foot hits the ground in his forward stride. The force is then recorded by pressure mapping. This shows which parts of the foot are most involved in the stride and transfer of weight. Force plate testing can help a pitcher develop a more natural stride and use the lower body to generate more velocity.

velocity
The speed of a pitch in baseball

Flexibility is vital to a pitcher's throwing motion. Pitchers who suffer from joint stiffness or range of motion problems may attend yoga classes to help improve their flexibility.

Learning to Throw Harder

Velocity is the holy grail of pitching. The first thing a scout looks for in a young pitching prospect is the speed of the pitcher's fastball. Although pitchers can work to develop fancy breaking pitches and changeups, veteran coaches have always claimed that throwing a lively fastball is a gift, not a skill that can be learned. However, that piece of received wisdom is being revised. Today there are more pitchers throwing fastballs at more than 90 miles per hour (145 kph)—and even more than 100 miles per hour (161 kph)—than ever before. The science of 3-D motion analysis and biomechanics is helping professional pitchers throw harder with less stress on their pitching arms. Whereas the ability to throw a baseball 95 miles per hour (153 kph) was once a rarity, now it is almost a requirement for pitchers in the major leagues. "There's tons of guys that throw 95-plus, and their average career is like a running back in the N.F.L.," says training consultant Kyle Boddy. "They pitch two or three years and then they're done."[13]

Boddy operates Driveline Baseball, a data-driven training center that serves as a biomechanics lab for pitchers. Driveline

Motion Analysis for Softball Pitchers

Just as in baseball, women's fast-pitch softball teams value speedy pitches that move in the strike zone. And just like their counterparts in baseball, female softball pitchers are turning to 3-D motion analysis and biomechanics to enhance their abilities. Many training services like P3 work with high school and collegiate softball pitchers on a regular basis.

In fast-pitch softball, the distance from the pitching rubber to home plate is less than in baseball—43 feet (13.1 m) compared to 60.5 feet (18.4 m). Yet the best pitchers in softball regularly deliver the ball at speeds of 70 miles per hour (112.7 kph) or more. Adjusting for distance, this is equivalent to a 100-mile-per-hour (161 kph) pitch in baseball. Plus, since the underhand throwing motion in softball is considered to place much less stress on the shoulder and arm than the overhand motion, softball pitchers work many more innings. An ace softball pitcher may complete two or more games in a single day, throwing more than one hundred pitches per game.

Some experts believe throwing too many pitches in a short span is still a bad idea for softball pitchers, especially young women in high school. Many coaches are turning to motion analysis to help their pitchers not only increase speed but also avoid injuries. According to Jackie Magill, who has coached many softball pitchers at the college level, "Sports science labs have studied the pitching motion and made discoveries about the physics of pitching that actually debunks some of our prior thinking."

Jackie Magill, "8 Incorrect Softball Pitching Mechanics," Softball Pitching Tools.com, June 23, 2018. www.softballpitchingtools.com.

uses 3-D motion analysis and biomechanical data about hip, trunk, and arm angles to improve pitch velocity. Driveline is part of baseball's revolution in pitch speed. The statistics site Fan-Graphs notes that the average MLB fastball in 2002 clocked in at 89 miles per hour (143.2 kph). By 2017 that number had risen to 92.8 miles per hour (149.3 kph), and it promises to keep going up. Pitchers who cannot throw heat in today's game often find themselves in danger of losing their job. "One hundred miles per hour is the new benchmark," says Tom House, who helps run camps and clinics across the country. "That's where the research is going."[14]

Trevor Bauer is one of Driveline Baseball's many success stories. In high school Bauer could manage only a mediocre 78-mile-per-hour (125.5 kph) fastball. To increase his velocity, Bauer worked with Ron Wolforth at the Texas Baseball Ranch. Eventually, he became a first-round draft pick and reached the major leagues. When his fastball began to fade in 2012, Bauer started training at the Driveline center with Boddy, who borrowed many of Wolforth's techniques. At Driveline, Bauer threw brightly colored PlyoCare balls of various weights, some lighter than the standard baseball and some heavier. These balls are designed to give pitchers a different tactile feel in the hand, to distance them from the anxiety of throwing a baseball. Bauer also did strength exercises and underwent several sessions with the 3-D motion-analysis cameras. After some adjustments to his throwing motion, Bauer was able to pitch with less effort and regularly reached 95 miles per hour (153 kph) with his fastball. "This is something the baseball world has roughly been doing forever: seeing mechanical flaws and using drills to try and correct for them," says Sam Briend, a performance analyst at Driveline Baseball. "With the biomechanics report, we just have a much more targeted approach."[15]

Bauer has been a reliable starter for the Cleveland Indians since 2015. He has joined a list of MLB pitchers, including the Miami Marlins' Dan Straily and the Detroit Tigers' Matt Boyd, who have added pop to their pitches with the help of Boddy and his

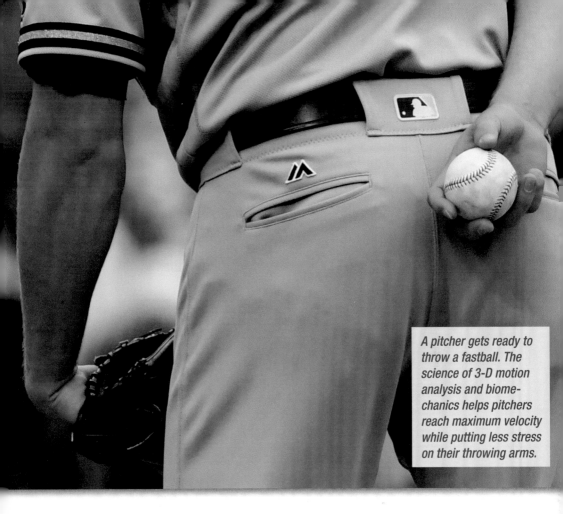

A pitcher gets ready to throw a fastball. The science of 3-D motion analysis and biomechanics helps pitchers reach maximum velocity while putting less stress on their throwing arms.

staff. And who knows? Hidden among the high school and college prospects paying to get the scientific treatment at Driveline might be baseball's next great strikeout pitcher.

Statcast and Perceived Velocity

Pure speed, measured in miles per hour, is not necessarily the best indicator of a strikeout pitch. More important is how fast the pitch *seems* to be traveling, as gauged by the batter's reaction time. MLB experts call this perceived velocity (PV). The difference between actual velocity and PV has to do with release point, or when the ball actually leaves the pitcher's hand.

In past years the PV effect was something batters talked about but could not explain. With Statcast, PV can now be measured

Designing the Perfect Curveball

The Pitching Lab at Rockland Peak Performance in Sloatsburg, New York, advises its clients on everything about spin—that is, the spin of a thrown baseball. Its 13,000-square-foot (1,208 sq. m) facility combines expert training techniques with the latest scientific approaches to pitching, including data analysis. Rockland trainers believe that the best approach to improving pitcher performance has to combine the art and the science of baseball. To do this, these experts look at spinning a baseball in as many ways as possible.

One cutting-edge tool at the Rockland Pitching Lab is the Rapsodo machine. As a client throws pitches, Rapsodo's tracking device captures a host of data about each pitch. The data flows to a digital dashboard on a computer tablet or PC. Among the metrics that Rapsodo collects about a pitch are spin rate, true spin rate, spin axis, and spin efficiency, as well as velocity, vertical drop, and horizontal drop. The data is stored for each session so that a client can follow his or her progress. Ultimately, all that data enables Rockland trainers to advise their clients about pitch design. This means adjusting the spin rate for curveballs and other off-speed pitches. "We do this by altering the grip on the ball, different mental and physical cues, finger positioning and action at release points among other things," says Robbie Aviles, a former pro pitcher who coaches at the Rockland Pitching Lab. With Rapsodo's data tracking and Aviles's expertise, state-of-the-art technology is apt to produce designer curveballs in the major leagues.

Robbie Aviles, "Analyzing Spin Rate and How to Incorporate It into Training Pitchers," Rockland Peak Performance, November 17, 2017. www.rocklandpeakperformance.com.

with great precision. Statcast not only records the speed of each pitch but notes the release point in relation to home plate. This data then is compared to the league average release point. As baseball journalist Spencer Bingol explains: "[PV is] basically a function of pitcher extension—if two relievers throw pitches at 100 mph, but one releases the ball a foot closer to home plate than the other, his pitch will reach home plate at a higher perceived velocity due to the batter having less time to react."[16]

Thus, a long-armed pitcher who lets the ball go farther in front of the pitching rubber will seem to be throwing harder. PV is responsible for the jump effect that makes some fastballs seem to explode out of the pitcher's hand. For example, at 6 feet 10 inches (208 cm), Baseball Hall of Famer Randy Johnson, a fire-baller to begin with, had one of the most unnerving PVs in base-ball history. And Statcast explains why.

Pitchers are learning to take advantage of PV, sometimes by bending the rules. In 2015 Miami pitcher Carter Capps achieved high PV numbers and great success out of the bullpen with an unusual delivery. Capps would push off with his back foot and literally take a jump step toward the batter before releasing the pitch. Since then MLB has outlawed Capps's approach. Others are achieving high PVs in a more conventional way, making use of their height and long arms. In 2018 the New York Mets' Jacob deGrom led the majors with a difference of 1.2 miles per hour (1.9 kph) between his PV and his actual fastball velocity. Team-mate Zack Wheeler was close behind with 1.1 miles per hour (1.8 kph). Not surprisingly, these two are among the best young pitchers in baseball.

The Importance of Spin Rate

Raw speed is only one weapon in a successful pitcher's arse-nal. The best pitchers are those who combine speed with ball movement. A pitch that comes in straight as a string—even a pitch over 90 miles per hour (145 kph)—is liable to be hit hard by a major league batter. But if a hurler can make the ball sink or fade or seem to rise, he has a much better chance of fooling the hitter. That is where a new scientific measurement like spin rate comes in.

Statcast's Doppler radar measures spin rate in revolutions per minute (rpm). The average spin rate for a four-seam fastball—a standard fastball with all four seams rotating in the air—is about 2,250 rpm. However, pitchers who achieve a much higher spin rate for a four-seamer tend to be good strikeout pitchers. As MLB.com analyst Mike Petriello explains:

> The reason why we care about spin in the first place is because it helps to define how a pitch can move. For example, high spin on a fastball helps the ball defy gravity for slightly longer than a pitch with average spin, and this is often referred to as a "rising fastball." That's a somewhat misleading name, because the ball doesn't really rise, it just falls more slowly than a hitter expects. But even if that's a difference of only a few inches, that can make all the difference as far as whether the batter makes square contact or misses entirely.[17]

Thus, a batter tends to swing under a fastball with a high spin rate, either missing entirely or hitting a lazy pop-up. In fact, high spin rate correlates with swinging strikes, the mark of a good strikeout pitcher. The Houston Astros' Justin Verlander and the Washington Nationals' Max Scherzer typically amass strikeouts with rising fastballs and high average spin rates. At the same time, two-seam fastballs, which have a lower spin rate than average, can also be very effective pitches. They tend to sink or tail off, leading the batter to pound the ball into the ground for easy groundouts.

Spinning a Curveball

Curveballs are slower pitches with lower spin rates than fastballs. Nonetheless, inability to hit a sharply breaking curveball has wrecked the careers of many promising hitters. With a spin rate averaging 1,500 rpm, an expert curveball can bend several inches to almost a foot (30 cm) horizontally or vertically. Statcast offers precise data on a curveball's speed, spin, and tilt (direction of spin leaving the pitcher's hand). A curveball's wicked movement is calculated according to laws of physics that take into account speed and spin. Pitchers who can spin their curves at more than 2,000 rpm are highly valued for the way the ball dances around a flailing bat. "I feel it come off my hand and I know it's most likely going to result in a punch-out [strikeout]," says Astros pitcher Lance McCullers, one of the best curveball pitchers in the majors. "Like, this is a really quality pitch."[18] MLB teams are experimenting with devices that can measure how different grips and finger positions on the ball can alter spin rate. Pitchers may one day be able to adjust the spin rate on their pitches with great confidence.

Scientific approaches like biomechanics and data analysis are changing the ways pitchers train and develop their skills. Three-dimensional motion analysis can help identify flaws in a pitcher's delivery, improve velocity, and relieve pressure on the throwing arm. Sophisticated data from Statcast, such as perceived velocity and spin rate, gives pitchers new tools to make them more effective. In order to throw faster and develop exotic breaking pitches, today's pitchers can rely on new technologies beyond anything their fathers' generation could have imagined.

CHAPTER THREE

A Scientific Approach to Batting

In a sport like baseball that reveres the record book, the home run is king. Home run records attract attention like no other feat. That is why the September 28, 2018, game in Boston between the hometown Red Sox and their longtime rivals, the New York Yankees, was so special. In the fourth inning, New York's Gleyber Torres smacked a two-run homer that gave the Yankees the all-time record for most home runs in a season, at 265. They ended the season with 267 home runs, a mark that only the Yankees themselves may be able to challenge. For a team known as the Bronx Bombers since the days of Babe Ruth and Lou Gehrig, it was no surprise that the Yankees were leading a resurgence in home run hitting throughout MLB. As slugger Giancarlo Stanton said upon joining the Yankees, "I feel sorry for the baseballs."[19] Moreover, like almost all the other MLB teams, the Yanks were relying on science and technology to boost their long-ball production.

The Difficulty of Hitting

With or without the help of science, hitting a baseball is one of the most difficult things to do in sports. The very best hitters in the big leagues fail two-thirds of the time. On average, a major league batter has about 125 milliseconds to assess the speed and location of an oncoming pitch. That is less than the time it takes to blink. He must decide whether to swing before the ball is even halfway to home plate. Meanwhile, the pitcher (with his own scientific approach) can resort to fastballs, changeups, curveballs that veer left or right, and pitches that dive straight into the ground at the last instant. Plus, many pitchers use elaborate windup motions to hide the ball and increase the deception. For a hitter, getting fooled—often embarrassingly so—comes with the territory. "It's difficult because guys in this league throw really hard and they're really, really good," says the Colorado Rockies' Daniel Murphy. "Guys are throwing aspirins at us."[20] When Murphy refers to aspirins, he is not talking about pain relief. He means that fastballs look like tiny white pills as they zip by.

Looked at scientifically, a major league batter's task can seem almost impossible. It takes one-tenth of a second for the brain to process what the eye sees. This lag time is crucial. By the time a batter begins to swing at a fastball, he is already acting on old visual information. However, science also reveals how batters succeed as often as they do. Not only do they rely on keen eyesight and hand-eye coordination, they also harness an ability to predict motion and trajectory (the path of a moving object). Vision scientists at the University of California–Berkeley have found that a mechanism in the visual cortex of the brain helps track fast-moving objects by mentally pushing them forward along the path they seem to be traveling. As lead scientist Gerrit Maus explains, "The image that hits the eye and then is processed by the brain is not in sync with the real world, but the brain is clever enough to compensate for that."[21] This predictive ability not only enables MLB batters to hit a fastball, it also allows ordinary people to avoid oncoming cars in traffic.

visual cortex
The part of the brain that receives and processes sensory information from the eyes

Focus on Exit Velocity

Today science promises to help MLB hitters gain an advantage. As with pitching, 3-D motion analysis and radar tracking are enabling batters to analyze all the aspects of hitting in greater detail than ever before. They use data to help them improve their technique at the plate. For example, Statcast measures the exit velocity of a baseball as it comes off the bat. The higher the exit velocity, the more likely it is that the hit ball will result in a double, triple, or home run. The highest exit velocity of any MLB home run in 2018 was 121.7 miles per hour (196 kph), achieved by the Yankees' Giancarlo Stanton. The blast also traveled 449 feet (137 m) from home plate. As Stanton's technique shows, hitting for power requires a hard swing that is

How to Hit a Fastball

Hitting a baseball traveling at 100 mph requires almost superhuman skill. At that speed, a pitched ball reaches the hitter in just 400 milliseconds (ms). If a batter takes 200 ms to react and 100 ms to swing the bat, that leaves 100 ms. Within that time frame, the brain has to track the ball's path, calculate its speed and direction, predict when and where it will cross the plate, and activate the muscles—all in an effort to connect bat and ball.

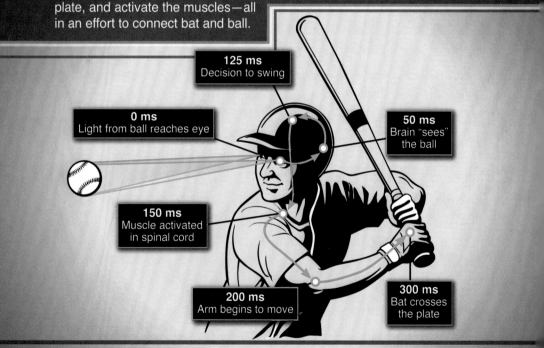

125 ms
Decision to swing

0 ms
Light from ball reaches eye

50 ms
Brain "sees" the ball

150 ms
Muscle activated in spinal cord

200 ms
Arm begins to move

300 ms
Bat crosses the plate

Source: Science NonFiction, "Hitting a Fastball Requires More than Just Quick Reactions," May 23, 2016. https://sciencenonfiction.org.

Using Statcast Data for Ballpark Design

Experts who design MLB ballparks are looking to Statcast for help in creating cutting-edge venues that cater to baseball's top hitters. In Tampa Bay, Florida, engineers at Walter P. Moore are making plans for a new domed ballpark in the Ybor City neighborhood. To start, they downloaded a torrent of Statcast data about balls hit inside Tropicana Field, the current ballpark. The data filled ninety columns on a spreadsheet. The engineers then used details about the speed and angle of 7,736 fly balls as they left the bat to create a computer model predicting the arc of each fly ball. They did a special analysis of balls hit by the New York Yankees' slugging duo of Aaron Judge and Giancarlo Stanton, since the division rival Yankees visit Tampa Bay for several games each season. "We wanted to make sure we caught any crazy outliers from the hardest hitters in baseball," says Aaron White, an engineer at Walter P. Moore.

The research paid off with some not-so-surprising results. Judge and Stanton hit balls so high and far that they occasionally struck the catwalks in the roof of the current Tampa Bay stadium. To avoid such outcomes in the projected new facility, the engineers raised the roof of the dome and eliminated the catwalks. Tampa Bay pitchers may have trouble keeping the Yankee sluggers from hitting home runs in the new ballpark, but at least the baseballs will not be grazing the stadium roof.

Quoted in Richard Danielson, "Rays Ballpark Engineers Computer-Modeled Fly Balls to Design a Roof That Would Stay out of Play," *Tampa Bay Times*, August 16, 2018. www.tampabay.com.

under control. "In order to get the ball to go farther, you have to make it come off the bat faster," says science writer Sara Chodosh, "and a key way to do that is to make the bat-ball collision as energy-efficient as possible."[22]

As it happens, the wooden bats used in MLB games are not great for energy efficiency. When a baseball strikes a wooden bat, it loses about half of its energy in compressing. As shown by super-slow-motion cameras, the ball actually squishes on contact to about half its width for one millisecond before bouncing back to full size. This occurs because

For safety reasons MLB hitters are required to use wooden bats that provide significantly less exit velocity than composite or metal bats. Players can increase their hitting power by choosing a bat with more weight in the barrel.

the solid wood of the bat cannot compress, forcing the ball to undergo all the compression during contact. Hitters could get more exit velocity if they used composite or metal bats, which are hollow inside. These bats actually compress a bit on contact and then bounce back, sending a charge of force into the ball like a trampoline effect. However, for safety reasons,

MLB outlaws composite or metal bats. The fear is that hollow bats would produce dangerous exit velocities—meaning line drives screaming at the pitcher's head. Some hitters have been known to cheat by hollowing out the barrel of a wooden bat to get this trampoline effect.

A legal way to get greater exit velocity has to do with choosing the proper bat. The best bat for power hitting has a certain so-called moment of inertia, which is the measurement of how the bat's mass is distributed. A slugger's bat should be weighted toward the barrel, or the end away from the handle. An end-loaded bat feels heavier and can be harder to swing, but it produces more exit velocity. "If swung at [the] same speed, the bat with the larger moment of inertia will hit balls faster," observes Dan Russell, a professor of acoustics at Penn State University who studies vibrations in baseball bats. "Moment of inertia matters way more than the weight, but no manufacturer lists moment of inertia, and I have no idea why. I've been asking that for 20 years."[23]

Testing bats for exit velocity calls for special technology. Both pro and collegiate teams can monitor exit velocity in batting practice with units such as FlightScope Strike, a 3-D Doppler radar setup that tracks the flight of a baseball or any moving object. It was originally designed for military purposes such as missile tracking. As it happens, Doppler radar is also good for tracking the high-flying moon shots of the Yankees' Aaron Judge and other sluggers. "It's sending out microwave signals, and then with the Doppler effect and the disturbance in the frequencies, we're able to detect the full flight of a projectile—whether it's a missile or a pitched or batted baseball,"[24] says David Mayberry, a baseball application specialist for Flight-Scope. Coaches and hitters receive exit velocity data from FlightScope Strike on a PC or tablet. This way they are able to test how different swing approaches affect exit velocity in real time. With practice it is hoped hitters will soon be launching missiles of their own.

Launch Angle for Power Hitting

Hitting a missile-like home run calls for the right launch angle. Here Statcast has brought about a major change in MLB by measuring the launch angle of a batter's swing. Launch angle is the vertical angle at which a ball leaves a player's bat. Many hitters are changing their swings and trying to launch the ball higher into the air. The result is fewer ground balls, more fly balls and extra base hits, including home runs. In fact, baseball is in the midst of a home run explosion. The 2017 season saw a record total of 6,105 homers in the major leagues. Although the 2018 total dropped off to 5,585, the trend toward swinging for the fences shows no signs of going away. Home runs keep the seats filled in MLB ballparks and help the top sluggers earn multimillion-dollar contracts.

As a result, launch angle has become almost an obsession for many big league hitters. A good example is Josh Donaldson, who recently signed a $23 million deal with the Atlanta Braves. After a mediocre stint in the minor leagues, Donaldson worked with a batting coach to develop an uppercut swing. As he learned to lift the ball, he watched more of his deep flies sail over the fence. He became a reliable slugger and won the American League Most Valuable Player Award in 2015. Donaldson's hitting philosophy is reflected in his tweet: "Just say NO . . . to ground balls."[25] Boston's J.D. Martinez used to marvel at how batters smaller than him could reach the fences more easily. He worked with private hitting instructors who urged him to rethink the mechanics of his swing. Now he focuses on lofting the ball as much as possible.

Many players have researched the best launch angles for success and try to incorporate that knowledge into batting practice. "I know 10 degrees is about the point where infielders cannot catch it," says Colorado Rockies second baseman Daniel Murphy. "And then 25, 27 is the sweet spot for home runs."[26]

mechanics
The motions involved in a particular activity

The Rise in Strikeouts

Just as Statcast data has helped fuel a surge in home runs, it has also brought a plague of strikeouts. The 2018 MLB season was the first in history to see more strikeouts than hits. The rise in strikeouts is part of a long-term trend, with MLB setting a strikeout record for the eleventh consecutive year. The growing rate of strikeouts has some observers worried about games getting longer with less action. Casual fans like to see the ball in play. As Crash Davis tells Nuke LaLoosh in the classic baseball movie *Bull Durham*, "Strikeouts are boring!"

The main culprit behind all those strikeouts is the data-based idea that hitting home runs and extra-base hits is the most efficient way to score runs. With even the scrawniest batters now swinging from the heels, it is no wonder strikeout totals are exploding. The trend also has baseball purists rolling their eyes. In the past, a hitter would shorten his swing with two strikes in order to make contact and avoid striking out. Nowadays few hitters change their approach regardless of the count.

So what is the solution? Two possibilities are lowering the pitcher's mound and reducing the number of pitchers on a roster. Lowering the mound would make it easier for batters to hit a flattened pitch squarely. With fewer pitchers on staff, batters would see a fresh pitcher less often. And perhaps a return to more balls in play and fewer strikeouts would help speed up the games.

Quoted in Tom Verducci, "There's Too Many Strikeouts in Baseball: Here's How to Fix the Problem," *Sports Illustrated*, June 14, 2018. www.si.com.

A Theory Backed by Statistics

The theory behind launch angle is nothing new. In his 1970 book *The Science of Hitting*, Hall of Famer Ted Williams explained the idea in simple terms: "The [pitched] ball angles down, not straight or up. You don't need calculus to see it. It's obvious. And it means the best way to hit it is to swing slightly up, not level or down. Meet it squarely along its path. They got that wrong for years, ever since Ty Cobb."[27]

What *is* new is the precision with which Statcast measures launch angle. Its TrackMan Doppler radar tracks the flight of the ball off the bat and instantly calculates the angle of exit. For comparison, MLB has guidelines for the launch angles of different kinds of contact. A ground ball is less than 10 degrees; a line drive is 10 to 25 degrees; a fly ball is 25 to 50 degrees; and a pop-up is greater than 50 degrees. Statcast even provides scatterplot graphs that show the likelihood of getting a hit for different launch angles and exit velocities.

scatterplot
A graph that has points bunched to show the relationship between two sets of data

The past few seasons have seen the average launch angle in MLB steadily climb from 10.5 degrees in 2015 to 12.4 degrees in 2018. (The average launch angle reflects the fact that every batter hits quite a few ground balls.) The Oakland A's Khris Davis, whose forty-eight homers led the majors, attacks pitches with a powerful uppercut. His average launch angle of 18 degrees ranked well above the major league standard. The A's used the science of exit velocity and launch angle to hit the third most home runs in MLB. The strategy also paid off in wins, as the A's made the playoffs for the first time in several seasons.

For all their potential benefits, the new power statistics can be deceiving. The Giancarlo Stanton homer that had the highest exit velocity in all of 2018 also had a launch angle of only 17.4 degrees. Hard-hit line drives and ground balls can still produce runs. And an uppercut swing can also result in lots of pop-ups and swings and misses. With all this in mind, a few hitting coaches are placing less emphasis on launch angle. They urge players to focus on a comfortable swing and solid contact, even if that means hitting fewer balls in the air. "As an instructor, you have to know the strengths and weaknesses of each of your players and what's going to work best," says Detroit Tigers' batting coach Lloyd McClendon. "When you talk about launch angle, for every five players that it works for, there's another five it doesn't work for. You have to be really careful about that and go about it the right way."[28]

The right launch angle is essential to hitting home runs. Boston Red Sox right fielder J.D. Martinez (pictured) reworked the mechanics of his swing to launch the ball higher and reach the fences more often.

A New Take on Batting Order

Another way data analysis has affected hitting is in the batting order. This is the order in which each team's hitters come to the plate. Throughout baseball history, managers have chosen for the leadoff spot a small, fast player who could hit singles, draw walks, and steal bases. The third, fourth, and fifth slots were reserved for the team's best hitters, with the idea that they could drive in the players ahead of them to produce more runs. Stat-based thinking, however, has turned the traditional batting order upside down.

Many managers now put their most productive hitters—usually in terms of OPS—at the top of the lineup. That way they will get the most possible at bats and have the most opportunities to deliver extra-base hits and drive in runs. In 2016 Houston Astros' manager A.J. Hinch had George Springer, a burly power hitter, bat leadoff for most of the season. "Some of the stereotypes that come with 'Is the leadoff hitter a small, scrappy, on-base machine?' versus me sending up a 6-foot-3, 225-pound George Springer, it might look different," says Hinch. "But what we're after is scoring the most runs and putting your most dangerous hitters to get the most at-bats is an effective way to do that."[29] Hinch's rethinking of his team's batting order helped the Astros win the 2017 World Series.

According to strict sabermetrics, batting order does not matter all that much. The number of extra at bats a power hitter might get by moving to the leadoff spot translates to only about forty or fifty in a season. However, that might be just enough of an advantage to win a division race or sneak into the playoffs as a wild-card team. "If you want to get a two- or three-win edge, it requires getting a very, very, very small edge in probably dozens of different situations," says baseball analyst Mitchel Lichtman. "Just to not do one because it's a very small gain, well . . . you never get your two or three extra wins."[30]

Data analysis has convinced most MLB teams that swinging for home runs and extra-base hits is the best way to maximize a team's offensive production. Statcast provides new metrics such as exit velocity and launch angle that help sluggers reach their potential. Managers have even revamped their batting orders to get more at bats for productive hitters. Due to breakthroughs in collecting data and crunching the numbers, the theory of hitting in baseball continues to undergo a radical change.

CHAPTER FOUR

Applying Science to Fielding and Baserunning

As Adrian Gonzalez of the New York Mets stepped into the batter's box, he looked out toward right field. That is the direction Gonzalez loves to pull the ball with his left-handed swing. But instead of the usual two infielders on that side of the field, the New York Yankees had stationed three. The third baseman was playing to the right of second base, while the second baseman had trotted out to shallow right field. Only the first baseman was in his usual spot. The center fielder and right fielder had both edged toward the right field line. The Yankees were stacking five defensive players on the right side in the expectation that Gonzalez would pull the ball that way. However, the veteran Gonzalez upset the Yankees' strategy. He drilled a ground ball the opposite way, down the third base line for a double. Gonzalez ended up stranded on second, but he had achieved a small victory. He had beaten the shift—and spoiled, for the moment, the Yankees' reliance on data and statistics.

A Major Impact

Few strategic changes have had such a large impact on MLB as the shift. Managers regularly stack their fielders on the batter's power side of the diamond. Teams use scatterplot data from Statcast about a hitter's history of batted balls to determine where he is most likely to hit the ball. Then they shift their fielders into the new positions each time that batter comes to the plate. Research indicates batters hit about 15 to 20 percentage points lower when faced with a shift.

The shift has proved especially effective in swallowing up ground balls. Time after time a hitter will smack a grounder that seems destined for a hit, only to have a shifted infielder snag it and throw him out. According to Kyle Seager of the Seattle Mariners, "It happens so many times now, where a ball would have been in the 4-hole [between first and second base], but that isn't there anymore. Or you hit a line drive up the middle, and the guy is standing there. It's kind of the new norm."[31] Daniel Murphy marvels at the speed with which the new strategy has taken hold. "It's actually been quite impressive to watch how quickly teams have adapted to the data they've got,"[32] says Murphy.

A pitcher can also do his part to make the shift work. With the aid of Statcast data about a batter's tendencies, the pitcher can throw to spots that increase the likelihood the batter will hit into the shift. "As hitters can attest, teams routinely pitch to the shift," notes baseball reporter Jerry Crasnick. "A pitcher is not going to throw soft stuff away to a left-handed hitter with the entire left side of the infield uninhabited."[33]

Teams vary as to how often they use the shift. The Houston Astros, for example, employ the shift more than any other team in MLB. In the 2018 season they shifted on more than 43 percent of their opponent's plate appearances. For certain power hitters like the Texas Rangers' Joey Gallo, the Astros actually played six players to the right of second base, an alignment they call the trapezoid defense. That left only one outfielder to patrol the entire left side of the diamond. Astros manager A.J. Hinch admits there is some gamesmanship mixed with the science of the shift. By moving their fielders to one side, the Astros hope to lure hitters into bad swings. "There's some psychological

gamesmanship
The art of using strategy to get an advantage psychologically

Baltimore Orioles coach Dave Cash makes a change to the lineup during a game. By using a hitter's batting history to determine where he is most likely to hit the ball, teams can shift fielders into new positions each time that player comes up to bat.

warfare that goes on," says Hinch. "It's like chess."[34] The strategy worked for the Astros: They won 103 games and finished first in the American League's West Division. However, the shift cannot make up for lack of talent in other areas. The Baltimore Orioles also resorted to the shift quite often and wound up mired in last place.

Drawbacks of the Shift

Like so many data-based changes to baseball, the shift has come under fire for its supposedly bad effects on the game. Critics insist, for example, that the shift only increases the modern hitter's urge to swing for the fences. Faced with extra fielders on their pull side of the field, batters often decide the best strategy is to hit the ball over them. This results in more fly balls but also more pop-ups and strikeouts—and a game with less action for the fans. Even MLB commissioner Rob Manfred has voiced his concern: "Take shifts. When they came, everybody said it was

Biomechanics of a Stolen Base

In the late innings of a close game, a stolen base can be the difference between winning and losing. David Kagan, a physicist at California State University at Chico and a huge baseball fan, has subjected the stolen base to scientific analysis. Kagan came up with a model for calculating the time it takes a runner to reach second base on a steal. The model includes five variables: the runner's lead off first base; his jump, or acceleration when he starts to run; the top speed he attains when sprinting to second; his deceleration, or rate of slowing down when he begins to slide; and the speed he is traveling when he reaches second base.

Kagan then turned to a math technique called a sensitivity analysis to see which variables are most important for success. Not surprisingly, he found that the runner's top speed is most important in determining base-stealing success. Second most important is the jump the runner gets. However, the third most important variable was unexpected. The runner's speed when he actually reaches second base is more important to success than his lead off first base. In other words, runners should try to maintain as much speed as possible when sliding. That is why runners often slide headfirst nearer to the base and grab for it as they slide by. Kagan's research shows why baserunners should worry less about a big lead and pay more attention to the biomechanics of their sliding technique.

common thought, 'People are going to learn just to go the other way.' But the fact of the matter is the human element took over, and what they decided to do was go over the top [rather] than go the other way."[35]

Many fans echo Manfred's point. They wonder why, when batters are confronted with a half-empty field, they do not simply punch the ball into the open area for an easy hit. Even a bunt down the line would do. However, players who try to beat the shift this way often fail. Few hitters in today's game can adjust their swings to hit the ball where they want—especially against 100-mile-per-hour (161 kph) fastballs. "The times I've thought about it and tried to go the opposite way, it didn't work out too well for me," says the Toronto Blue Jays' Justin Smoak. "My swing gets long. I start rolling over to second, rolling over to first. I feel like it's better to just try to hit it hard and not worry where it goes."[36]

Measuring Speed and Reaction Time

Wherever they are stationed, fielders must react quickly to a batted ball in order to make a catch or prevent an extra-base hit. Here again, players are turning to data analysis to help them get an extra edge. A good example is the Minnesota Twins' center fielder Byron Buxton. Already an excellent defensive player, with blazing speed and uncanny instincts, Buxton decided he still had room for improvement. Working with Statcast data and Twins coaches, Buxton found that his first step when the bat struck the ball was not quick enough to suit his high standards. In the off-season he focused on an aspect of the game that until recently had never been measurable.

Statcast offers data on fielding that is just as extensive as the pitching and batting numbers. The radar tracking system records how long it takes a fielder to react to a ball and how fast he runs to intercept it. If a fielder can reduce his reaction time, he can get to balls more quickly and record more outs. Statcast also offers unusual new statistics such as catch probability. This calculates the chance an average fielder has of catching a certain batted ball. The system even measures the velocity and accuracy of throws from the outfield. With Statcast, a fielder's performance can be analyzed in great detail. As sportswriter Jared Diamond explains:

probability
The chance that a certain outcome will occur

> Because of Statcast we know that on one leaping catch last month, Buxton ran 68 feet and reached an elite top speed of 29.7 feet per second. On another play last week, we know Buxton tracked down a ball that the average

outfielder would fail to catch 82% of the time. That figure is based on how much ground Buxton covered (112 feet), how much time he had to cover it (5.4 seconds) and the direction he ran (back and toward right-center), all information Statcast monitors. All told, according to Statcast, Buxton has saved 24 outs over the average outfielder this season. Nobody else has even topped 17.[37]

Buxton's stat-based work in the off-season has paid off with spectacular defense. He now jets off after the ball at the crack of the bat. Now and then his Statcast-measured reaction time has hit a *negative* three-hundredths of a second. This means Buxton sometimes gets a jump on the ball even before it hits the bat. "I picked up on the numbers and I was like, 'Well, I can be better than this, I can do this better," says Buxton. "So I started picking out the small things that I felt like I could get a little better at."[38] Teammates like pitcher Kyle Gibson appreciate Buxton's efforts and his value to the team. Gibson likes to slip into the video room under the stadium during games to check the Statcast numbers on Buxton's latest defensive gem.

Taking the Best Path to the Ball

Elite fielders like Buxton also can be evaluated by another defensive statistic: route efficiency. This compares the path a fielder actually takes to reach a ball's landing point with the ideal path. Route efficiency is calculated as a percentage of this ideal path. For example, in 2015, when the Houston Astros' George Springer robbed the Texas Rangers' Leonys Martin of a potential game-winning grand slam home run, Statcast showed his route efficiency to be an astonishing 99.1—almost perfect. In other words, if Springer had taken one false step, he could not have caught the ball and saved the game for the Astros.

Starting with the 2017 season, MLB has replaced route efficiency with catch probability as a fielding metric. MLB believes fans care more about comparing fielding performance with what

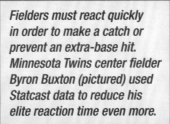

an average fielder can do than with some geometrically perfect path to the ball. Catch probability is more straightforward and easier to understand. Another problem with route efficiency is that the most efficient route is not always the best way to make a play. If an outfielder circles behind a sacrifice fly in order to set himself for a throw to home plate, Statcast penalizes him for taking an indirect path. Still, if he throws out the runner, he made the right choice, regardless of the stats.

Catch probability also can indicate just how far above average a difficult fielding play is. In June 2018 the Los Angeles

Wearable Devices for Performance Data

Via Statcast cameras and radar tracking, MLB collects tons of data about players' speed, reaction time, and throwing ability, among other skills. Now MLB is collecting even more data, including information about fatigue and stress level, from wearable devices that can be used during games. For instance, in an agreement with WHOOP, a Boston-based tech company, MLB has approved the wearing of biometric monitors on and off the field. The wrist-strap monitors provide data about heart rate, heart rate variability, and body temperature. In-game data from the monitors are off limits to team staff and players, but the data is available to both after the game. Future wearable devices will record levels of hydration, muscle fatigue, and oxygen in the blood.

Players are not required to wear the WHOOP monitors on or off the field, but many choose to wear them not only in games but twenty-four hours a day. The data they provide on sleep and recovery helps these professional athletes maintain their bodies at a peak performance level. Soon such wearable devices may become an unobtrusive part of a player's lifestyle. According to baseball writer Stephanie Springer, "A more tech savvy player might try to incorporate wearable technology into his own routine, without attracting notice, as sports technology looks more and more like regular athletic wear."

Stephanie Springer, "An Update on Wearable Baseball Technology," *Hardball Times* (blog), August 7, 2018. www.fangraphs.com.

Angels' Mike Trout, one of baseball's best defensive players, tore off after a ball hit to the fence in left center by the Rangers' Delino DeShields. Based on the direction of the hit and the distance to the wall, Statcast rated the probability of an average fielder catching the ball as only 19 percent. Yet Trout is anything but average. He was able to make a sensational grab, having run an almost perfect route of 104 feet (31.7 m) at 29 feet (8.8 m) per second. It was, according to MLB stats, Trout's unlikeliest catch of the Statcast era. He also made it look easy, snagging DeShields's drive at full speed without having to dive or bang into the wall.

Angels coach Dino Ebel is not surprised by the Statcast data on Trout. He knows how quickly and efficiently Trout reacts to a long drive. "The thing about Mike this year, when the ball's hit, he's moving, where even if it's not hit to him, it's the first step," says Ebel. "The most important thing that Mike is doing is in his mind he wants to catch every ball that's hit to him and hit in the gaps, and he's going for it."[39]

Gauging Base Runner Speed

Baseball is a game of inches, with several plays each game decided by a base runner's speed—or lack of speed. Statcast reveals that the MLB average for sprint speed is 27 feet (8.2 m) per second. (Miles per hour is considered a poor measuring tool for sprinting speed.) The Twins' Byron Buxton led all of baseball in 2018 with a sprint speed of 30.5 feet (9.3 m) per second, 3 feet (91.4 cm) per second faster than the average. As Mike Petriello notes on MLB.com, "While three feet per second may not sound like much, if you were to maintain that speed for four or five seconds, suddenly you're talking 12–15 feet. It can be the difference between being safe or out or not even trying. . . . Olympian [sprinter] Usain Bolt, by comparison, has reached up to 37 feet per second in his first 40 meters."[40]

acceleration
The capacity to gain speed in a short time

Armed with Statcast data about speed and acceleration, faster players work to develop an even better approach. The key is reaching top sprint speed as quickly as possible. This means exploding out of the batter's box to beat out a slow infield roller or tearing toward home plate to score on a sacrifice fly. To improve acceleration, players build fast-twitch muscle fibers in their lower body. This is done with resistance running—straining to run while pulling a weight or facing an opposing force. In the past some players would run in water for resistance. Today they run in a wind resistance chute, which

Toronto Blue Jays infielder John McDonald (left) runs resistance sprints during spring training. Resistance running builds fast-twitch muscle fibers in the lower body, increasing a player's acceleration.

adds from 15 to 30 pounds (6.8 to 13.6 kg) of resistance. Some speedsters work out by pulling a sled filled with sand. They can vary the load depending on their leg strength. Some run on an electric treadmill that is turned off, forcing the tread to turn with each stride. With effort, a runner can accelerate to a sprint at 20-second or 30-second intervals. "Resistance training like this will help your reaction time from the plate onto the base path," says Josh Maio, cofounder and head coach of Gotham City Runners in New York, "and it will also build strength in your hips to keep you out of the trainer's office."[41]

The rise of data analysis in MLB has caused teams to rethink how they position their players in the field and defend against different batters. The shift, in which extra players are stacked to one side of the field, enables teams to tailor their defense to a batter's hitting history. Statcast also records a fielder's response time and the efficiency of his path to the ball. Its measurement of each player's speed on the base paths prompts players to work on lower body strength for more explosive acceleration. Although there is no substitute for speed and skill in baseball, these new metrics help teams gain a competitive advantage over a long season.

CHAPTER FIVE

Using Science to Avoid Injuries

Twenty-five-year-old Daniel Gossett, a promising pitcher for the Oakland Athletics, was making only his fifth start of the 2018 season in Kansas City. After a strong five innings in which he gave up only one run, Gossett left the game with soreness in his pitching elbow. A magnetic resonance imaging (MRI) scan showed a strain of his flexor muscle. When the pain in his elbow worsened while Gossett was tossing some soft pitches several days later, he began to worry. A consultation with the team physician revealed the elbow had more damage than first indicated on the MRI. The meeting ended with the word Gossett did not want to hear: *surgery*. Within days he had his ulnar collateral ligament (UCL) surgically repaired. The next twelve months would be filled with rehab routines and worries about the future. At least Gossett could rely on advice from other young pitchers on the A's staff. After all, he was the fourth A's pitcher to require the same type of season-ending surgery in 2018. A's manager Bob Melvin tried to put the best face on things. "Obviously, it's unfortunate," says Melvin. "These are injuries that keep you out for a while. . . . To have this many guys go down certainly hurts us, but it gives someone else an opportunity."[42]

An Epidemic of Tommy John Surgeries

Of all the players on a baseball team, pitchers are most likely to be injured. Throwing a baseball overhand at tremendous speed places a great deal of strain on a pitcher's shoulder and elbow. As Gossett can attest, the elbow is especially vulnerable. His teammates Kendall Graveman, Jharel Cotton, and A.J. Puk would agree. These four are just part of the epidemic of so-called Tommy John surgeries that is sidelining pitchers throughout MLB. Young pitchers know what might be in store when soreness in the elbow refuses to go away, but the reality can still be a shock. "I didn't really prepare myself, but I knew that [surgery] could be part of it," says Gossett. "I mentally took a step back and realized that could be a part of it, and we'll attack it how we can."[43] Gossett, like his recovering teammates, is expected to miss the entire 2019 season.

Hundreds of professional pitchers have had Tommy John surgery at some point in their careers. The stress of whipping the pitching arm forward to deliver a 95-mile-per-hour (153 kph) fastball or slider can, over time, shred the band of fibers that forms the UCL in the elbow. The UCL is a small triangular ligament, about 1 by 2 centimeters, that connects the upper arm's humerus bone with the lower arm's ulnar bone. The Tommy John procedure replaces the damaged ligament with a healthy tendon from the player's arm or leg. The surgery is named for the Dodgers left-hander who was the first to undergo the experimental UCL reconstruction in 1974. The procedure was so successful that John pitched for fourteen seasons and recorded 164 of his 288 career wins after it was done.

orthopedic
Having to do with the branch of medicine concerned with correcting problems of bones or muscles

Although young players today shudder at the thought of Tommy John surgery, it actually has been a career saver for many pitchers. "I've met a lot of players from the 1960s, and when pitchers like Sandy Koufax suffered his ligament injury to his elbow, his career was over," says Timothy Kremchek, an orthopedic surgeon based in Cincinnati, Ohio. "If we had the technology to [diagnose] injuries such as his that we have now, and the ability to assess the injury, it wouldn't have been the 'death sentence' it was to the career of pitchers as it was back in the 1960s."[44]

The Injury Nexus for Pitchers

Then and now, MLB owners and general managers have been keen to protect their investment in players. Young pitchers like the A's quartet are considered to be in a particularly risky pe-

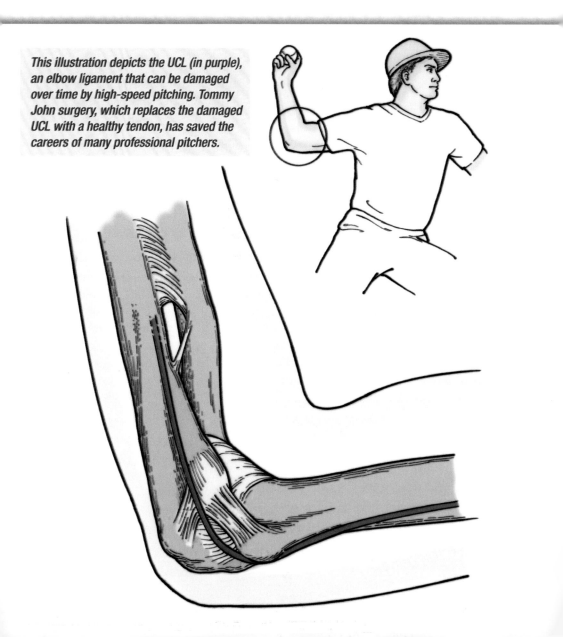

This illustration depicts the UCL (in purple), an elbow ligament that can be damaged over time by high-speed pitching. Tommy John surgery, which replaces the damaged UCL with a healthy tendon, has saved the careers of many professional pitchers.

riod called the injury nexus. The concept comes from a report written in 2003 by the statisticians Will Carroll and Nate Silver. According to Carroll and Silver, the injury nexus is the time in a player's late teens or early twenties when the added pitching workload in professional baseball can cause elbow soreness or worsen a condition that is already there. In these years a young pitcher is most likely to sustain a career-altering injury to his pitching arm. Many of the most serious injuries involve the UCL.

The annual number of pitchers in both the major leagues and minor leagues who must undergo Tommy John surgery has been declining some but remains high. More than 143 pitchers had it done in 2015, while the number fell to less than 100 in 2018. Seventeen of those were pitchers in the major leagues. Experts differ on the reasons for the decline but find it encouraging all the same. Overall, Tommy John surgeries cost MLB teams hundreds of millions of dollars in costs and lost revenue.

Preventing Pitching Injuries from Overuse

With economic incentives so high, MLB teams are desperate to curb the rate of Tommy John surgeries and other serious injuries to pitchers. One way that teams protect their pitchers is to carefully monitor their workload, by keeping track of innings worked and pitch count in games. The idea is to increase workload gradually so as not to strain a young pitcher's arm. Many coaches and scouts say the elbow problems with today's pitchers begin in high school with year-round throwing. "Why is everyone coming forth with all the arm injuries?" asks Terre Haute North Vigo High School coach Fay Spetter. "We played baseball during baseball season. We played football during football and basketball during basketball. Our arms were not moving forward 12 months out of the year. I just truly believe rest is the key to that. You don't need to be throwing in November, December and January."[45]

When young pitchers go from amateur baseball to professional leagues, their workload can increase in a hurry. From throwing around one hundred innings a year, they sometimes go up to nearly two hundred. All MLB teams now monitor innings jumps from one year to the next as a major red flag for possible injury. A jump of 30 percent or more is considered the danger zone for arm fatigue. "You see the wear and tear of a big innings jump show up the next year," says baseball analyst Tom Verducci. "The symptoms could be reduced velocity or shoulder inflammation, not necessarily a major injury. Innings limits have evolved as more data become available, but developing young pitchers and keeping them healthy remains one of the biggest mysteries in baseball."[46]

inflammation
The body's reaction to injury or infection, leading to swelling, redness, and often pain

Pitch count—or number of pitches thrown by a single pitcher—has become such a common statistic that MLB television broadcasts show it onscreen. And ball clubs have become more proactive in tracking pitching data. From 2014 to 2018, the average pitch count per start fell from ninety-six to eighty-nine. The number of starting pitchers to log at least two hundred innings was cut almost in half, from twenty-eight in 2015 to only fifteen in 2018.

Teams use data analysis to set pitch count limits for various pitchers depending on their conditioning and experience. In general, a starting pitcher is removed from a game when he nears one hundred pitches. However, a statistic that may be more important to pitcher fatigue than raw pitch count is the so-called stress inning. A stress inning is one in which a pitcher gives up several walks or hits and ends up throwing lots of pitches in a short time. Fatigue and anxiety can disrupt a pitcher's throwing mechanics and increase the chance of arm injury. The St. Louis Cardinals, for example, take a pitcher out if he throws more than thirty-five pitches in one inning.

Talented young pitchers have so much long-term value that teams sometimes sacrifice immediate success in order to protect them for the future. One of the most famous cases is that of Stephen Strasburg, a fireballing young right-hander for the Wash-

.250	4	I	0	I		
2015 SEASON						
AVG	**AB**	**H**	**HR**	**RBI**		
.275	571	157	28	90		

34 NOAH SYNDERGAARD

GAME			**101** MPH	**POSTSEASON**		
PITCHES	STRIKES	BALLS		ERA	SO	WH
8	8	0	PITCH SPEED	0.00	1	0.0

LA LOVES OCTOBER

1	2	3	4	5	6	7	8	9	R	H	E	BALL STRIKE

Pitch count, or the number of pitches thrown by a single player, has become a common statistic in Major League Baseball. Teams use pitching data, shown here on an MLB scoreboard, to help reduce overuse injuries in pitchers.

ington Nationals. Led by the then twenty-four-year-old Strasburg, whose elbow had already been repaired with Tommy John surgery, Washington had the National League's best record in the 2012 season. Yet sticking to a preseason analytics-based limit of 160 innings for Strasburg, General Manager Mike Rizzo shut him down for the playoffs. "We've got a lot of bright and happy days ahead of us watching Stephen Strasburg pitch,"[47] Rizzo said at the time. Without Strasburg, however, the Nationals failed to reach the World Series. Years later the team still has not made the Fall Classic.

A Stress-Free Pitching Motion

The most successful big league teams focus on more than workload to protect their pitchers. Another crucial concern is the pitcher's mechanics. To avoid shoulder and elbow injuries, pitchers must

The Pitch Smart Campaign

When the number of UCL surgeries continued its alarming rise in 2014, MLB decided to act. Its new strategy reached down to pitchers in high school and Little Leagues. In partnership with USA Baseball, the governing body for amateurs, MLB set up the Pitch Smart campaign to protect young pitching elbows. The campaign includes a website that offers guidelines for coaches, players, and parents. The guidelines set limits for how much young pitchers should throw and recommends ways to prevent elbow injuries. For example, the website provides pitch counts and rest schedules tailored to different age groups. The goal is to prevent elbow soreness from becoming a chronic problem for young pitchers whose arms have not developed fully.

Dr. Glenn Fleisig, research director of the American Sports Medicine Institute, worked with MLB to launch the Pitch Smart campaign. Fleisig's group had conducted a decade-long research project on five hundred young pitchers to study the causes of elbow injuries. The project found that those who pitched more than one hundred innings a year were three times more likely to need elbow surgery by their twentieth birthday. MLB and USA Baseball used Fleisig's results to design their pitch count rules for young players. "Our results indicated the increase in youth baseball injuries [was] due to year-round play and overuse," says Fleisig. "The professional injuries today are, in fact, occurring to the first generation of players who grew up playing baseball year-round." Fleisig hopes his work will reduce the need for Tommy John surgery throughout baseball.

Quoted in MIT Sloan Sports Analytics Conference, "Q&A: Dr. Glenn Fleisig on Tommy John Surgery Prevention and Myths." www.sloansportsconference.com.

develop a throwing motion that reduces stress on the pitching arm. While each pitcher's throwing motion is different, all should include basic principles of torque and weight shift to relieve stress on the pitching arm. This is where technology can play an important role. "You can't clone everybody. How they pitch is how they pitch," says Colton Turner, a pitcher in the White Sox farm system for up-and-coming players. "But at the same time, if the science finds something that could lead to injury and you can help them out, the pitcher has to know it."[48]

With the wear and tear of throwing nearly one hundred pitches averaging 90 miles per hour (145 kph) over the course of three hours every five days, it is a wonder that MLB pitchers survive the season. But biomechanics and motion-capture technology can help pitchers eliminate flaws in their delivery and avoid chronic arm soreness. Kitman Labs, a sports science technology company, offers a full menu of high-tech analysis for pitchers. Kitman

Young pitchers have long-term value, so teams sometimes sacrifice immediate success in order to protect them for the future. One case is that of Stephen Strasburg (pictured with his pitching progression), a pitcher for the Washington Nationals, whose elbow had already been repaired with Tommy John surgery when he was twenty-two years old.

engineers use radar systems to track a pitcher's throwing motion and release point and to diagnose early signs of fatigue. Motion-capture sensors enable coaches to break down the delivery in detail. If a pitcher's arm is too high or too low at some point, that frame can be flagged on a tablet or laptop for correction.

Medical experts say the main cause of pitching injuries is fatigue. Dr. Glenn Fleisig notes that when a pitcher gets tired, his mechanics change. He tends to shorten his stride and lower his elbow. This puts extra strain on the UCL. Such changes may be all but impossible to see with the naked eye, but tracking tech-

Not Just for Pitchers

Tommy John surgery is known as the pitcher's surgery. But torn UCL ligaments can afflict players at other positions, too. Corey Seager, the all-star shortstop for the Los Angeles Dodgers, makes hundreds of throws across the diamond every day. In late April 2018, however, Seager began to feel twinges in his throwing elbow, then a general numbness. A couple of hard throws brought a sharp pain. He hoped it was only some inflammation, but an MRI revealed a tear in his elbow ligament. Seager had to undergo surgery, putting him out for the rest of the season. For good measure, he also had hip surgery to correct a nagging problem in August. He had to sit and watch as the Dodgers rolled to the National League pennant and the World Series.

Dr. Tommy John, whose father lent his name to UCL surgery, says position players like Seager face just as difficult a rehab as pitchers. A shortstop's elbow has to be especially strong to cope with the demands of daily stress. As John explains, "He has to make throws off balance, off one foot, in an array of mechanically disadvantageous positions, falling down, short armed, side armed with no spine tilt, poor grips, spinning through the air etc. His surgical recovery time should be looked at no differently than their most valuable arm on their pitching staff."

Quoted in Matt Borelli, "Dr. Tommy John Talks Corey Seager's Recovery, UCL Surgeries in 'Minimize Injury, Maximize Performance: A Sports Parent's Survival Guide,'" Dodger Blue, July 3, 2018. www.dodgerblue.com.

nology can bring them to light. "Two pitchers who both throw 100 pitches may exhibit very different elbow and shoulder damage because of their mechanics," says Fleisig. "The best way to understand and measure a pitcher's mechanics is to conduct a full biomechanical analysis."[49] Pitchers also benefit from biometric strength and conditioning programs. These can develop hip and hamstring flexibility and increase lower-body strength. Such workouts show their value in late innings when fatigue threatens to disrupt a pitcher's delivery.

A Sleeve to Measure Elbow Strain

Fatigue and elbow strain have always been subjective things that are hard to measure. Now, however, pitchers at all levels are using a new sensor technology that provides concrete data on elbow stress. The Motus electronic sleeve is a smart device that a pitcher can slip over the elbow during practice. The purpose of the Motus sleeve is to monitor the workload of the pitching elbow, collect data, and signal problems that could lead to injury. With each pitch that a pitcher throws, gyroscopes inside the Motus sensor start to spit out data about arm speed, forearm rotation, and elbow torque. The latter measurement could prevent scores of Tommy John surgeries by raising a red flag.

gyroscope
A device that helps a sensor measure direction and distance

Fleisig sees the Motus sleeve as a breakthrough in biometric tech. He explains:

> Motus' technology is not just spitting out the acceleration of your elbow—it's actually using biomechanics equations to calculate the *force* on your elbow. Let's say you have two pitchers on a team and they both throw 65 miles-per-hour. And they both throw 70 pitches [in a game] and they go home and one kid says, "Hey, my elbow hurts."

Wouldn't it be nice to know that one kid probably put more *force* on his arm per throw? Motus gives you that—the forces that are relevant to injury.[50]

The Motus sleeve can also benefit a player with no elbow problems. Dan Straily, a starting pitcher with the Miami Marlins, used workouts with the sleeve to guide his rehab for a troublesome shoulder. When he increased the velocity of his pitches, the sleeve showed no added stress on his elbow. Confident that his elbow and throwing motion were sound, Straily focused on building up his shoulder to weather an MLB season.

Fear of UCL injuries continues to prompt teams to use science and technology to protect their young pitching arms. Everything from data-based restrictions on pitches and innings to biometric analysis of pitching motions helps keep pitchers healthy and ready to take the mound. Recent inventions like the Motus sleeve can even monitor elbow stress in real time. Technology is one of the most valuable medical aids available to today's players.

SOURCE NOTES

Introduction: A Game of Numbers

1. Quoted in Greg Beacham, "After Counsell Uses Miley as Decoy, Brewers' Pen Cracks Late," *AP News*, October 17, 2018. www.apnews.com.
2. Quoted in Bob Nightengale, "*USA TODAY* Survey: MLB Power Shift Has Managers' Salaries in Free Fall," *USA Today*, August 27, 2018. www.usatoday.com.
3. Quoted in Brian Costa and Jared Diamond, "The Downside of Baseball's Data Revolution—Long Games, Less Action," *Wall Street Journal*, October 3, 2017. www.wsj.com.

Chapter One: Statcast and the Data Revolution

4. Quoted in Bob Hille, "The Whole Story of Trevor Story's Statcast-Blasting Night," *Sporting News*, September 6, 2018. www.sportingnews.com.
5. Quoted in Dave Sheinin, "These Days in Baseball, Every Batter Is Trying to Find an Angle," *Washington Post*, June 1, 2017. www.washingtonpost.com.
6. Michael Lewis, *Moneyball: The Art of Winning an Unfair Game*, New York: Norton, 2003, p. 67.
7. Lewis, *Moneyball*, p. 141.
8. Tom Ward, "How Theo Epstein Wins (and How You Can Too)," *Forbes*, October 24, 2016. www.forbes.com.
9. Quoted in Aaron De Smet and Jeff Hart, "A View from the Front Lines of Baseball's Data-Analytics Revolution," *McKinsey Quarterly*, July 2018. www.mckinsey.com.
10. Quoted in Geoff Guerin, "Red Sox Respond to Adviser Bill James' Comments 'Players Are Not the Game,'" *Bosox Injection*, November 12, 2018. www.bosoxinjection.com.

Chapter Two: Making Pitchers More Effective

11. Quoted in Peter Baugh, "St. Louis Native Brian DeLunas Steers Successful Ship of Mariners Relievers," *St. Louis (MO) Post-Dispatch*, July 13, 2018. www.stltoday.com.

12. Quoted in Greg Johns, "Mariners Hire DeLunas as Bullpen Coach," MLB.com, December 4, 2017. www.mlb.com.

13. Quoted in Tyler Kepner, "Velocity School: Where Pitchers Pay to Throw Harder," *New York Times*, September 14, 2017. www.nytimes.com.

14. Quoted in Kepner, "Velocity School."

15. Sam Briend, "Pitching Assessments and Changing Mechanics," Driveline Baseball, October 30, 2018. www.driveline baseball.com.

16. Spencer Bingol, "Statcast Data: The Top Differences in Actual and Perceived Velocity," *Beyond the Box Score* (blog), SB Nation, April 12, 2016. www.beyondtheboxscore.com.

17. Mike Petriello, "Why Spin Rate Matters for Fastballs," MLB .com, January 3, 2017. www.mlb.com.

18. Quoted in Tom Verducci, "Forget Velocity, the Curveball's Resurgence Is Changing Modern Pitching," *Sports Illustrated*, May 23, 2017. www.si.com.

Chapter Three: A Scientific Approach to Batting

19. Quoted in Coley Harvey, "Yankees Hit Nos. 265, 266 to Set Single-Season Home Run Record," ESPN, September 29, 2018. www.espn.com.

20. Quoted in Alex Speier, "More and More Players Practicing What Ted Williams Preached," *Boston Globe*, March 17, 2017. www.bostonglobe.com.

21. Quoted in Barnet-Dulaney-Perkins Eye Center, "How Baseball Players See a Fastball," March 31, 2017. www.goodeyes .com.

22. Sara Chodosh, "The Ultimate Guide to Hitting a Home Run," *Popular Science*, March 29, 2018. www.popsci.com.

23. Quoted in Chodosh, "The Ultimate Guide to Hitting a Home Run."

24. Brandon Hall, "Why Every Baseball Player, Regardless of Age, Should Care About Their Launch Angle and Exit Velocity," Stack, March 29, 2018. www.stack.com.

25. Quoted in Todd Kortemeier, "Have Your Say: Should Players Care About Launch Angle?," TheSeason, April 4, 2018. http://theseason.gc.com.

26. Quoted in Neil Greenberg, "The Statistical Revelation That Has MLB Hitters Bombing More Home Runs than the Steroid Era," *Washington Post*, June 1, 2017. www.washingtonpost.com.

27. Quoted in Speier, "More and More Players Practicing What Ted Williams Preached."

28. Quoted in Chris McCosky, "Tigers' McClendon: Launch Angle Works, but Not for All," *Detroit (MI) News*, February 23, 2018. www.detroitnews.com.

29. Quoted in Zach Kram, "The Batting Order Revolution Will Be Televised," Ringer, March 31, 2017. www.theringer.com.

30. Quoted in Kram, "The Batting Order Revolution Will Be Televised."

Chapter Four: Applying Science to Fielding and Baserunning

31. Quoted in Jerry Crasnick, "MLB Hitters Explain Why They Can't Just Beat the Shift," ESPN, July 10, 2018. www.espn.com.

32. Quoted in Crasnick, "MLB Hitters Explain Why They Can't Just Beat the Shift."

33. Crasnick, "MLB Hitters Explain Why They Can't Just Beat the Shift."

34. Quoted in Gerry Fraley, "Astros' Manager A.J. Hinch Admits There Is 'Some Psychological Warfare' in Shifting Against Joey Gallo," SportsDay, May 12, 2018. http://sportsday.dallas news.com.

35. Quoted in Anthony Rieber, "For Hitters, Adjusting to Beat the Shift Is No Easy Task," *Newsday*, June 17, 2018. www.news day.com.

36. Quoted in Arden Zwelling, "Why Don't Players Try to Beat the Shift? It's Just Not That Simple," *Sportsnet*, July 18, 2018. www.sportsnet.ca.

37. Jared Diamond, "How Tracking Technology Helped Baseball's Best Fielding Outfielder," *Wall Street Journal*, September 20, 2017. www.wsj.com.

38. Quoted in Diamond, "How Tracking Technology Helped Baseball's Best Fielding Outfielder."

39. Quoted in Ben Lindbergh, "Mike Trout Is on His Way to the Best Season Ever," *Ringer*, June 4, 2018. www.theringer.com.

40. Mike Petriello, "Sprint Speed Metric Now Tracks Baserunners," MLB.com, June 26, 2017. www.mlb.com.

41. Quoted in Gavin Evans, "Ask the Pros: How to Shave Seconds off Your Base Running," *453 and a Half* (blog), Dick's Sporting Goods, April 17, 2015. http://blog.dickssporting goods.com.

Chapter Five: Using Science to Avoid Injuries

42. Quoted in John Shea, "Daniel Gossett Is 4th A's Pitcher This Year Requiring Tommy John Surgery," *SFGate*, July 31, 2018. www.sfgate.com.

43. Quoted in Eric He, "Gossett to Lean on Teammates After TJ Surgery," MLB.com, August 4, 2018. www.mlb.com.

44. Quoted in John Wagner, "Tommy John Surgery a Common Part of Baseball," *Toledo (OH) Blade*, August 10, 2018. www .toledoblade.com.

45. Quoted in Bob Cook, "Why Young Arms May Burn Out Even with Pitch-Count Limits," *Forbes*, April 24, 2017. www.forbes .com.

46. Tom Verducci, "The 2018 Year After Effect: Which Young Pitchers Are at a Heightened Risk for Injury?," *Sports Illustrated*, February 19, 2018. www.si.com.

47. Quoted in Adam Kilgore, "Stephen Strasburg Shut Down for the Season," *Washington Post*, September 8, 2012. www .washingtonpost.com.

48. Quoted in Ray Glier, "Science of Baseball Evolving: Help Pitchers Avoid Injuries," *USA Today*, June 13, 2017. www.usatoday.com.

49. Quoted in MIT Sloan Sports Analytics Conference, "Q&A: Dr. Glenn Fleisig on Tommy John Surgery Prevention and Myths." www.sloansportsconference.com.

50. Quoted in Ben Berkon, "Biomechanics and the Youth Pitching Epidemic," *Vice Sports*, April 7, 2016. https://sports.vice.com.

Books

Russell A. Carleton, *The Shift: The Next Evolution in Baseball Thinking*. Chicago: Triumph, 2018.

Michael Lewis, *Moneyball: The Art of Winning an Unfair Game*. New York: Norton, 2004.

Ben Lindbergh and Sam Miller, *The Only Rule Is It Has to Work: Our Wild Experiment Building a New Kind of Baseball Team*. New York: Holt, 2017.

Rob Neyer, *Power Ball: Anatomy of a Modern Baseball Game*. New York: Harper, 2018.

Ben Reiter, *Astroball: The New Way to Win It All*. New York: Crown Archetype, 2018.

Travis Sawchik, *Big Data Baseball: Math, Miracles, and the End of a 20-Year Losing Streak*. New York: Flatiron, 2016.

Internet Sources

R.J. Anderson, "How Statcast Has Changed MLB and Why Not Everybody Seems All That Happy About It," CBS Sports, June 6, 2017. www.cbssports.com.

Paul Folkemer, "Stats All, Folks: A Look at Catch Probability and Outs Above Average—and Why Cedric Mullins Is a Huge Addition," BaltimoreBaseball.com, August 17, 2018. www.baltimorebaseball.com.

Tom Goldman, "What's Up Those Baseball Sleeves? Lots of Data, and Privacy Concerns," NPR, August 30, 2017. www.npr.org.

Neil Greenberg, "The Statistical Revelation That Has MLB Hitters Bombing More Home Runs than the Steroid Era," *Washington Post*, June 1, 2017. www.washingtonpost.com.

Mike Petriello, "9 Things You Need to Know About the Shift," MLB.com, May 16, 2018. www.mlb.com.

Websites

Baseball Prospectus (www.baseballprospectus.com). Baseball Prospectus covers every aspect of data analysis in baseball. It includes articles, podcasts, statistical analysis tools, and the latest research on baseball data and its uses.

Bill James Online (www.billjamesonline.com). This website is run by Bill James, whose ideas about sabermetrics and baseball statistics have had a huge effect on the game. The site features current articles about baseball stats, book reviews, and rankings of players.

Driveline Baseball (www.drivelinebaseball.com). Driveline Baseball is one of the foremost centers for cutting-edge baseball training and coaching. The Driveline website includes sections on training technology in baseball, coaching tips, blogs, and the latest research in biometrics.

MLB.com (www.mlb.com). This is the official website of Major League Baseball. MLB.com is constantly updated with articles and features about all aspects of baseball, including Statcast and data analysis. The site also includes a section on Pitch Smart, the initiative to help youth pitchers protect their arms.

INDEX

Note: Boldface page numbers indicate illustrations.

Aaron, Hank, 7
acceleration, defined, 53
American League Championship Series (2018), 9
American League Most Valuable Player Award (2015), 40
analytics
  data for, 6–7, 13–16
  defined, 7
  examples of use of, 6, 8
  slowness of games and, 9
"aspirins." *See* fastballs
Aviles, Robbie, 30

Baer, Larry, 9
ball movement, 31–33
ballparks, designing, 37
Baltimore Orioles, 47
Baseball Info Solutions, 17
bats, 37–39, **38**
batting
  difficulty of, 34–35
  efficiency of bat-ball collision, 37
  home runs
    increase in, 40
    launch angles and, 42, **43**
    longest, 10
    Yankees record for, in one season, 34
  order, 43–44, **47**
  the shift and, 45–49, 55
  strikeouts, 32, 41
Bauer, Trevor, 28–29
Beane, Billy, 15–16
Benintendi, Andrew, 9
Bingol, Spencer, 30

biomechanics
  defined, 22, 23
  of pitching, 22–25, 62–65, **63**
  of stolen bases, 48
Boddy, Kyle, 27–29
Bolt, Usain, 53
Boston Red Sox
  Beane and, 16
  Epstein and, 18–19
  in 2018 American League Championship Series, 9
Boyd, Matt, 28–29
Bregman, Alex, 9
Briend, Sam, 28
Bronx Bombers (New York Yankees), 34
Bull Durham (movie), 41
Buxton, Byron, 49–50, **51,** 53
By the Numbers (James), 18

Capps, Carter, 31
Carroll, Will, 59
Cash, Dave, **47**
catch probability, 49–53
chiropractic medicine, basis of, 23
Chodosh, Sara, 37
Cleveland Indians, 28–29
Cotton, Jharel, 57
Counsell, Craig, 6
Crasnick, Jerry, 46
curveballs
  biomechanics and, 22, 23
  designing perfect, 30
  spinning, 32–33

data
  for analytics, 6–7, 13–16
  baseball salaries and, 13
  captured by Rapsodo machine, 30
  computer technology and, 13
  previous use of, 7

spin rates, 31
suppliers, 17
technology to capture, 11–12, **15,** 19, 41–42
wearable collection devices, 52, 65–66
See also Statcast
Davis, Khris, 42
deGrom, Jacob, 31
DeLunas, Brian, 22, 23–24
DeShields, Delino, 52
Diamond, Jared, 49–50
Diaz, Edwin, 22, **24**
DiMaggio, Joe, 7
Dipoto, Jerry, 23–24
Donaldson, Josh, 40
Driveline Baseball, 27–29

Ebel, Dino, 53
energy efficiency of bats, 37–39
Epstein, Theo, 18–19
exit velocity, 36, 39

FanGraphs (statistics site), 28
fastballs
    hitting, 35, **36**
    "rising," 32
    two-seam, 32
    velocity of, 11, 28
fast-pitch softball, 27
fielding, **51**
    base runner's speed and, 53–54
    catch probability, 49–53
    route efficiency, 50–53
    the shift and, 45–49, 55
    ulnar collateral ligament injuries, 64
Fleisig, Glenn
    on biomechanics of pitchers, 64–65
    on Motus electronic sleeve, 65–66
    Pitch Smart campaign, 62
    speed of shoulder rotation of pitcher, 22–23
flexibility, 25, **26**
FlightScope Strike, 39
Fontenot, Gregory, 20

force plate testing, 25

Gallo, Joey, 46
gamesmanship, defined, 46
Giambi, Jason, 15–16
Gibson, Kyle, 50
Goldbeck, Graham, 17
Golden State Warriors, 20
Gonzalez, Adrian, 45
González, Carlos, 10
Gossett, Daniel, 56–57
Graveman, Kendall, 57
gyroscope, defined, 65

Hatteberg, Scott, 16
Hinch, A.J., 44, 46–47
home runs
    increase in, 40
    launch angles and, 42, **43**
    longest, 10
    Yankees record for, in one season, 34
House, Tom, 28
Houston Astros
    2017 World Series championship, 20, 44
    in 2018 American League Championship Series, 9
    use of the shift by, 46–47

inflammation, defined, 60
injuries
    fielding, 64
    pitching, 56–59, **58,** 61, 64–65
    preventing
        biomechanics and, **63,** 63–65
        Motus electronic sleeve and, 65–66
        Pitch Smart campaign, 62
        workload monitoring, 59–61, **61**
injury nexus, described, 58–59
Inside Edge, 17

James, Bill
    adoption of data analysis techniques of, 15–16

development of data analysis and, 13–14
Epstein and, 18–19
on replacement of players, 21
Jarvis, Sarah, 25
John, Tommy (baseball player), 57
John, Tommy (doctor), 64
Johnson, Randy, 31
Judge, Aaron, 37

Kagan, David, 48
Kitman Labs, 63–64
Koufax, Sandy, 57
Kremchek, Timothy, 57–58

launch angles, 40–42, **43**
Lewis, Michael
on Beane's use of James's approach, 15–16
book by, 16, 20
on statistics as misleading, 13
Lichtman, Mitchel, 44
Los Angeles Dodgers, 6, 64
Luhnow, Jeff, 20–21

Maddon, Joe, 7
Magill, Jackie, 27
Maio, Josh, 54
managers, use of analytics by, 6
Manfred, Rob, 47–48
Martin, Leonys, 50
Martinez, J.D., 40, **43**
Maus, Gerrit, 35
Mayberry, David, 39
McClendon, Lloyd, 42
McCullers, Lance, 33
McDonald, John, **54**
mechanics, defined, 40
Melvin, Bob, 56
Micheli Center for Sports Injury Prevention, 24–25
Miley, Wade, 6
Milwaukee Brewers, 6, **8**
MLB Advanced Media, 17
MLB.TV, 17
moment of inertia, 39

Moneyball: The Art of Winning an Unfair Game (Lewis), 16, 20
Motus electronic sleeves, 65–66
Murphy, Daniel
on fastballs, 35
on launch angles, 40
on the shift, 46
on use of analytics, 11

National Basketball Association (NBA), 20
National League Championship Series (2018), 6, **8**
New York Yankees, 34
1977 Baseball Abstract (James), 14

Oakland Athletics (A's), 15–16, 17, 42, 56–57
OPS statistic, 14
orthopedic, defined, 57

PECOTA (Player Empirical Comparison and Optimization Test Algorithm), 19
perceived velocity (PV), 29–31
Petriello, Mike, 32, 53
Phelps, David, 23
pitch count, 60, **61**
PITCHf/x, 19
pitching, **8, 24**
biomechanics of, 22–25, 62–65, **63**
curveballs, 30, 32–33
fastballs
hitting, 35, **36**
"rising," 32
two-seam, 32
velocity of, 11, 28
injuries to ulnar collateral ligament, 56–59, **58**, 61, 64–65
injury prevention
biomechanics and, **63**, 63–65
Motus electronic sleeve and, 65–66
Pitch Smart campaign, 62
workload monitoring, 59–61, **61**

to the shift, 46
softball, 27
strikeouts, 32, 41
Pitch Smart campaign, 62
pitch-tracking system, 19
Premier Pitching and Performance
   (P3), 23, 24–25
probability, defined, 49
Puk, A.J., 57

Rapsodo machine, 30
"rising fastballs," 32
Rizzo, Mike, 61
Roberts, Dave, 6
Rockland Peak Performance Pitching
   Lab, 30
route efficiency, 50–53
Russell, Dan, 39
Ruth, Babe, 7

sabermetrics
   adoption of, 15–16
   batting order and, 44
   development of, 13–14
   spread of, 17–18
scatterplots, defined, 42
Scherzer, Max, 32
School of Advanced Military Studies
   (Fort Leavenworth, Kansas), 20
Science of Hitting, The (Williams),
   41
scouts, 16–17, **18**
Seager, Corey, 64
Seager, Kyle, 46
Seattle Mariners, 22
sensitivity analysis, 48
sensors, defined, 11
shift, the, 45–49, 55
shortstops and ulnar collateral
   ligament injuries, 64
Silver, Nate, 19, 59
sliding techniques, 48
Smoak, Justin, 48–49
Society for American Baseball
   Research (SABR), 14
softball pitchers, 27

Spetter, Fay, 59
spin rates, 31–33
Springer, George, 44, 50
Springer, Stephanie, 52
spring training, 53–54, **54**
Stanton, Giancarlo, 34, 36–37, 42
Statcast
   annual data storage, 7
   data captured by, 10–11
      exit velocity of ball off bat, 36
      fielder's reaction time, 49
      launch angle of a batter's swing,
         40, 41–42
      perceived velocity, 29–30
      runner's speed and acceleration,
         53
      spin rate, 31
      strikeouts and, 41
      velocity and accuracy of throws
         from outfield, 49
   equipment used, 11–12, **15,**
      41–42
   longest home run, 10
   MLB Advanced Media and, 17
   using, for ballpark design, 37
statistician, defined, 14
statistics
   analytics and, 7
   batting order and, 43–44
   to help prevent injuries, 60, **61**
   as misleading, 13
   NBA use of, 20
   on-base percentage versus
      batting average, 14
   See also data captured by under
      Statcast
stereoscopic, defined, 13
stereoscopic cameras, 12
St. Louis Cardinals, 60
stolen bases, 48
Story, Trevor, 10, 11
Straily, Dan, 28–29, 66
Strasburg, Stephen, 60–61, **63**
stress inning, 60
strikeouts, 32, 41
Suárez, Andrew, 11

Tommy John surgeries
    pitchers and, 57–59, 61
    shortstops and, 64
Torres, Gleyber, 34
TrackMan Doppler radar, 11–12, 41–42
training, 53–54, **54**
trapezoid defense, 46
Trout, Mike, 52–53
two-seam fastballs, 32

ulnar collateral ligament (UCL)
    pitchers and, 56, 57–59, **58,** 62, 64–65
    shortstops and, 64
US Marine Corps base (Quantico, Virginia), 20

velocity
    choosing bats for greater exit, 39
    defined, 25
    exit, of ball off bat, 36, 39

    of fastballs, 11, 28
    increase in, as requirement for pitchers, 27
    perceived, 29–31
    of softball pitches, 27
Verducci, Tom, 60
Verlander, Justin, 32
visual cortex of brain, 35

Walter P. Moore, 37
Ward, Tom, 18
Washington Nationals, 60–61
Wheeler, Zack, 31
White, Aaron, 37
WHOOP, 52
Williams, Ted, 41
wind resistance chutes, 53–54, **54**
Wolforth, Ron, 28
Woodruff, Brandon, 6, **8**

yoga classes for flexibility, 25, **26**

PICTURE CREDITS

ABOUT THE AUTHOR

John Allen is a writer who lives in Oklahoma City.